MW01516203

A Shepherd's

HEART

101 MUSINGS ON THE PSALMS

PASTOR TERRY JANZEN

Copyright © 2024 by Terry Janzen

All rights reserved. No part of this publication may be reproduced, distributed, or transmitted in any form or by any means, including photocopying, recording, or other electronic or mechanical methods, without the prior written permission of the publisher, except in the case of brief quotations embodied in critical reviews and certain other noncommercial uses permitted by copyright law. For permission requests, write to the publisher, addressed "Riverside Community Church," at the address below.

Riverside Community Church
2329 Fremont Connector
Port Coquitlam BC, Canada V3B 0M3
www.rside.ca

Some scriptures are taken from the Holy Bible, New International Version®, NIV®. Copyright © 1973, 1978, 1984, 2011 by Biblica, Inc.™ Used by permission of Zondervan. All rights reserved worldwide. www.zondervan. com The "NIV" and "New International Version" are trademarks registered in the United States Patent and Trademark Office by Biblica, Inc.™

Some scripture quotations are taken from the King James Version. Public domain.

Thank you...

To my inspirational wife and beautiful life partner, Ingrid, for her faithful, unwavering encouragement to finish well.

To my three children, Torrey, Brody and Cassidy for so generously teaching me about life; Torrey, in particular, for the initial read through of this book.

Ben, JJ and Poppy: more precious life lessons.

Michelle Pride for capably compiling the original devotional.

Cheryl Liggins for encouraging me to resurrect the project, and for a second read through.

Reema Weglo for her skillful and enthusiastic efforts with design, and to get this book over the finish line.

And to the beautiful, warm people of Riverside Community Church for granting me the privilege of real-time practice to become a real, live pastor!

PREFACE

This devotional book is my gift to the Church that I have loved and served; from its birth in 2011, through the physical moving from one location to another, through the peculiar challenges of the pandemic, until today as I transition from the role of capital P "Pastor" to small p "pastor". Actually, I should correct that first line: OUR gift to the Church, as unmistakably and without exception, my wife Ingrid has, just behind the Lord Himself, made all of this possible, even enjoyable! This simple book is OUR gift to our beloved Riverside.

For a little context, it was largely written during the pandemic, as a way of trying to stay a bit more tangibly connected, in the face of some of the mandated isolation we all experienced.

As with most of what we do, and indeed, how we "pastor", it is conversational in nature. We hope it feels like us having a conversation about God with you, over a cup of coffee. It's nothing fancier or more profound than that. It reflects the way we have tried to pastor; simply, kindly, and genuinely; you'll also note some references to the rhythms and routines of pastoral work-preaching, praying, counselling, and the like.

The format copies the brilliantly simple SOAP model, popularized by Pastor Wayne Cordero of New Hope Christian Fellowship Church in Honolulu.Our prayer is that God uses His Word, through our experience as pastors, to draw you deeper into His loving embrace. May God richly bless you as you listen in to "A Pastor's Heart".

HOW TO USE THIS BOOK

As mentioned earlier, the format of these devotional musings is based on Wayne Cordeiro's SOAP model; each individual segment begins with a Scripture reference, followed by an Observation or two, followed by an Application concluding with a Prayer. S. O. A. P.—get it?

It does not follow a "one per day" pacing (though that is not discouraged!); it is more of an ongoing, uninterrupted "eat until you're full" approach. We think it's probably best engaged when you have adequate time to think and ponder. Jotting your thoughts and prayers down in the spaces provided is probably helpful as well.

It is our sincere hope that it will increase your love for, and dependence on, God's Word; that it will sharpen your listening ear to the voice of the Spirit; that it will stimulate your hunger for friendship with Jesus, long after these musings are forgotten.

Throughout "A Shepherd's Heart", I reference a colour-coding method that I have consistently used for many years, and through numerous Bibles.

If you're interested, very simply, here's how it works:

Through the use of a pre-determined guide of seven topics (you can name as many or as few as you like—I settled on seven), pencil crayon colours (they bleed through pages less than highlighters) are assigned to each topic.

Every time one of those topics is encountered, I simply colour over the words or phrases to highlight it.

My topics/colours look like this:

- ◆ Yellow: the character/nature of God
- ◆ Orange: the character/nature of Jesus
- ◆ Turquoise: the character/nature of Holy Spirit
- ◆ Red: Christian living
- ◆ Light green: a promise of God
- ◆ Dark Green: Faith principles
- ◆ Purple: leadership

There is no right or wrong way to do it—no exact numbers or best colours or frequency of colouring. It is entirely up to you. (For a teeny bit of context, most pages in my Bible have some colouring, but not every page.)

And, after years and years of practicing, I still find instances where I think "How on earth did I miss that?"

I hope you find this helpful.

Be blessed (and have fun!) while you study God's Word.

ONE

COMING HOME

SCRIPTURE ▶ Read Psalm 1.

OBSERVATION ▶ The other day I happened to find myself near my childhood home, so I detoured a little bit and drove into my old neighbourhood. Though everything seemed somehow smaller and closer than I remembered, which I suspect is common enough, what I was most impacted by was the general sense of warm familiarity I felt. I parked in front of our old house (not for too long, as that might arouse suspicion) and reflected on special moments, memories, both joyous and sorrowful, and I let the past wash over me. That profound sense of being home and of being secure was as wonderful as it was comforting. That's very close to the feeling I get when I begin reading the Psalms. I can't tell you how many times across the years of my life I have read the familiar opening lines: "Oh, the joys of those who do not follow the advice of the wicked, or stand around with sinners, or join in with mockers." This is then followed by more very helpful directives: to learn the importance of taking delight in the law of the Lord, which results in deep-rooted, prosperous spiritual health! An added layer of comfort is then administered, and this is probably quite specific to me, as pastor of a church whose identity was originally communicated by a startlingly similar verse in Jeremiah 17, "They are like trees planted along the riverbank, bearing fruit in each season. Their leaves never wither, and they prosper in all they do." (v8) Maybe now you can understand a bit better where that beautiful sense of familiar comfort and security comes from in my life and story.

APPLICATION ▶   But that's my story. What about you? What kind of story is God composing in and through you? What passages has He used in shaping you, and what discoveries await you as we journey through the Psalms together? I genuinely hope that I might have the honour of partnering with the Lord, even just a little, in the development of your incredible, unique story. So, let's sit down together and enter the vast and varied world of the Psalms; a world that covers every emotion, every trial, every joy and every sorrow known to the human experience. May you also discover what the psalmist did: "How precious are your thoughts about me, O God. They cannot be numbered!" (139:17) Now, that sounds like a warm and comforting invitation to me.

PRAYER

Our prayer is a simple one, Lord. To know You better, to love You more completely, to experience You more actively. Only You can produce these delights in us, Lord, so we're humbly asking: Do in us the best You have to offer. Thanks in advance.

Be blessed and encouraged, dear friends...

TWO

BEING CLOSE TO GOD

SCRIPTURE ▸ Read Psalm 2.

OBSERVATION ▸ I don't typically view my walk of faith as formulaic. Most of my personal spiritual journey is experienced relationally, with elements of method and corresponding disciplines thrown in alongside. I recognize that this approach might not work for everyone, but I'm just trying to be honest when I share that. Having said that, this particular passage is somewhat unique to me, in that the first thing I notice is actually a pattern, or at least an order of steps that provide spiritual direction. This can be super helpful, for I suspect that there are moments in anyone's spiritual journey in which a simple "ABC" user's manual can be beneficial, if not downright relieving! Let me explain: Verses 1-6 describe a chaotic world. Can you recognize it? The ultimate point is not the state of the world, that's obvious. The focal point is God's position in relation to the chaos all around us; the visual image is meant to help us with perspective. "The One who rules in heaven laughs…" This is a poignant reminder that no matter how desperate the world's condition is, God is still firmly and capably in control. His laughter indicates how ultimately untroubled He is by world events. Again, it is about perspective. The next couple of verses (6-9) add another dimension to the emerging pattern: relationship.

The same God who rules the world invites us into a close relationship. In the case of the kingly psalmist, he describes a father/child closeness. We know from the rest of the Bible that we are also entitled to that type of privileged status, by virtue of what Jesus has done on our behalf (for further study and clarification, have look at John 15:15, 2 Corinthians 6:18, Hebrews 10:10-22 for starters). So, we can have a close relationship with the Heavenly Father, the same Almighty God who is in control of all things.

The third step in our little guide is simply a response to the first two and answers the inevitable "what's next?" question; it's found in verses 10-12. So, what's next? Serve and submit, with joy. That may sound a little counter-intuitive, but it is a regular, inescapable staple of the Christian life. In order to partner well in relationship with God, we must lay down our will, our desires and our plans. There is no other way. The beautiful, perhaps unexpected result is joy. The joy of walking out life with the Lord, who, if He is capable of managing the world, is certainly capable of lovingly guiding His children, right?

APPLICATION⟩   Write out this simple pattern, something like this (it might end up sound suspiciously like a prayer!): "A"—Father, You are firmly in control of everything, big or small… "B"—You invite me into a loving, warm relationship, and so… "C"—I submit to Your best in my life. Teach me how to do this, because sometimes it's a hard thing to do. Oh, and fill me with Your joy as I serve you…

PRAYER⟩
See above!

THREE
THE SLEEP PSALMS

SCRIPTURE ▶ Read Psalm 3,4,5, & 6.

OBSERVATION ▶ I have often referred to this little group of chapters as "the sleep psalms". In the midst of them, quietly inserted, almost unnoticed, are references to sleep, to lying in bed, either calmly sleeping or when anxiety and worry crowd out restfulness, from night to morning. In the end, all these thoughts and corresponding imagery are covered by the assurance of God's tender care and comfort, much like a warm duvet on a cold night. Let's have a look at them all together, as we construct a picture of the Lord's presence, even in something as basic as our sleep. The first "sleep" reference is found in 3:5: "I lay down and slept, yet I woke up in safety; for the Lord was watching over me." Chapter 4 follows with: "In peace I will lie down and sleep, for you alone, O Lord, will keep me safe." Let me interject, just for a moment: At stressful and difficult times in my life, I have tried to let these passages simply "settle" over me, mostly as an expression of faith, choosing to believe that God is kindly attentive to my struggles. I don't view them as a magic wand or an instant solution; indeed, I have experienced nights in which sleep did not come, easily anyway, as I tossed and turned with worried and anxious thoughts. However, I can say with certainty that the Lord has faithfully watched over me. In fact, the most profound thing I take away from these scriptures is that our Father loves us so much, and in such detail, that he actually cares about our sleep and rest. I find that a truly comforting reality. Chapter 5 continues the theme with a reference to morning, and the quite natural expression of prayer, sometimes following a particularly difficult night. Aside from being a great directive in the life of any believer, praying in the morning has a way of stabilizing things, and bringing a healthy perspective in the light of a new day. Take note that verse 3 ends with the expectation of the Lord responding to our prayers.

APPLICATION ▶ I've never been one to quantify my spiritual health and growth by the amount that I read. For me, it's much more about the quality of my reading, and the thoughtfulness and attentiveness that I contribute to the process. Maybe a relatively slow and steady read (and re-read) of these 4 chapters would be in order, especially before bedtime and in the morning. You could throw in a reading of the account of David's anguishing story, just to help with some context. (2 Samuel 16-18)

PRAYER

Very simply: "But you, O Lord, are a shield around me; You are my glory, the One who holds my head high. I cried out to the Lord, and He answered me from His holy mountain." (3:3,4)

Rest well, dear friends.

FOUR

GRANDEUR OF CREATION

SCRIPTURE ▸ Read Psalm 8.

OBSERVATION ▸ There are times in my life when I enjoy the sense of feeling really small. Not always, but certain times for sure. I've recently had that sensation a couple of times: sitting in the presence of the red rocks of Sedona, Arizona. Standing in the middle of seemingly endless rows of grapevines overlooking Skaha Lake in BC's interior. A slow drive up the magnificent coastline of the Old Island Highway, dotted with its tiny towns, rocky beaches and oyster farms. I had that same sensation as I read Psalm 8 today; small, but not invisible, humbled, yet uplifted. This passage has a remarkable way of delivering healthy perspective, of clarifying the roles that God and I play, as well as how we partner together.

Verse 1 and 2 set the stage: talk about contrast between bigness and smallness! All the way from "Your glory is higher than the heavens" (really big!), to "You have taught children and infants" (really tiny!). That chorus repeated over the next couple of verses, from an awe-inspiring glimpse into God's creative genius in the crafting of the night sky (v3) (I saw that, too, in the desert skies of Arizona), to the astonishing concepts of God's thinking and purpose-filled plans and intention regarding interacting with human beings (v4-6).

APPLICATION I feel that this particular devotional needs to be a little more weighted toward application, though the application need not be complicated or only found in exotic locations. Maybe it's as simple as something like this: gazing upward while standing under the branches of a tree (when was the last time you were overwhelmed at how incredible a tree actually is?), pausing to enjoy the wonder of a sleeping child, making a trip to a body of water to consider that incredible act of creation. A quietly breathed prayer, while remembering that a God as big as ours lovingly partners with individuals as tiny as we are. Wow.

PRAYER

I guess we just did that, but in case you missed it, let's try this:

O Lord, our Lord, Your majestic name fills the earth" (1) (and fills my heart, too). Amen.

FIVE

GOD, WHY DO YOU HIDE?

SCRIPTURE ▶ Read Psalm 10.

OBSERVATION ▶ I'd like to start this devotion with a troubling thought, one that many believers are quick to ignore, or pretend that it doesn't exist, as though somehow its acknowledgement equates with a lack of faith and a lack of character. It's a thought that everyone has had, including Jesus Himself. If you don't believe me, take a moment to pause this conversation and flip over to Matthew 27 or Mark 15 and have a look.

I'm writing, of course, about the common human experience of feeling abandoned by God. Consider the anguish in the psalmist's voice: "O Lord, why do You stand so far away? Why do You hide while I'm in trouble?" (v1) I think it's important not to rush into the rest of this passage, to skim over this painful moment, scanning ahead to come to a safe and satisfactory conclusion—we'll get to those things eventually, as future readings in the Psalms will attest. Let's take a deep breath and linger in this raw moment for a little while. If you can't find it in yourself to trust me, trust the Lord—it's going to be okay! The reason it's important to not ignore that feeling is that it's a significant reality in the faith-journey of our lives; to do so robs us of an integral and necessary component in the process of deeply rooted faith. I once heard faith compared to the activity that takes place in a fitness centre. Muscles, as the illustration goes, only grow strong when faced with opposition and resistance. Lifting weights that stretch oneself to the limit, a place where discomfort and even pain exist is the whole point of strength training. To only lift weights that are easy to manage, require no real effort, are safely within one's capabilities, is pointless, and produces very little of real significance.

Can you see the parallels to the faith-journey? How often have we attended church, performed the outward signs of devotion and dedication, when on the inside feeling distant and abandoned? The short answer is: often, probably more frequently than I'd like you to know. Now, that's not to say I should abandon all faith disciplines the moment difficulties arise. That would be foolish and sad. Rather, there will be times when I do feel what the psalmist was expressing, and yet I choose to keep moving forward, incrementally and stumbling though it may be. So, it's a reality of faith, that both faith and doubt can exist side-by-side. Or maybe, I should say, they must. As we will discover, and as you will discover, God is capable of managing our doubt. Even by the end of this chapter, after a lengthy litany of complaints about of the character of his enemies, the author begins sowing the seeds of faith again: "Lord, You know the hopes of the helpless. Surely You will hear their cries and comfort them." (v17)

APPLICATION This is a moment that really requires respectful thoughtfulness. I don't write these things cavalierly or unkindly. I write them because I feel our faith is better served by being honest and forthright—when things are going wonderfully well, or when we languish in seasons of disappointment and doubt. So, maybe the application is really one of simple honesty.

I recently was in contact with a friend of deep faith and character who was undergoing very painful trials, on numerous fronts. I encouraged her that it was alright to say it, in ages-old partnership with those who have gone before us: "O, Lord, why do You stand so far away? Why do You hide when I am in trouble?" As we wait for clarity, or explanation, or maturity, or whatever we feel we need to wait for, the roots of our faith gradually strain downwards, growing deeper and stronger, able to withstand the next time when life's circumstances conspire to make us feel abandoned by God, whenever that may or may not come. (The author brings these feelings up again as soon as chapter 13!)

PRAYER

Lord, I lift up those who are feeling abandoned. It's a real feeling, though it is just that—a feeling. I pray for resilience and courage, for unshakable commitment to You, even though the ground around us may feel like it's crumbling. Ultimately, I pray for faith in You and Your character. You promised to never leave us or forsake us, and so, I pray that those realities will strengthen us moving forward. Grow deep, roots of faith...

SIX

THE LORD IS JUST

SCRIPTURE ▶   Read Psalm 11.

OBSERVATION ▶   I believe it was C.S. Lewis who wrote something along these lines: "It's not God who is on trial. It's us..." It's so easy to forget that, isn't it? Especially when life gets difficult, in our search to make sense of things, we often quickly turn to holding God and His character up for scrutiny, to question Him and demand that He give account for Himself. I suspect we've all done that on occasion, most often and simply in the form of "why?" Psalm 11 approaches difficult circumstances by a different route. The very first verse begins with a sweeping declaration, evidently given in the face of a direct challenge. Note the interplay: "I trust in the Lord for protection (there's the statement).

So why do you say to me, "Fly like a bird to the mountains for safety!" (That's the response; it almost sounds like we've entered a heated conversation mid-sentence!) To me, this is the essence of faith. Really, the starting point, the foundation: a declaration. Now, I realize that over the course of a lifetime, similar statements will be made and re-made. Seldom would it take the form of one singular utterance, spoken with such dedication and intensity that it was good for all time! It's true that there may have been a significant first time that it was expressed, and I suppose it's possible that it could be the one and only time that was needed, such was the depth of the 'settled-ness', but for me anyway, it has been a pretty regular part of my prayer and worship experience. Understand that repeating that commitment to trust in the Lord probably most benefits the one making the declaration. God is not needy, desperate to hear praise and receive adulation, as though He's had a bad day, and will feel better about Himself should enough of His followers say enough nice things to Him. Ridiculous! No, He is perfect and needs nothing. It's us (remember Mr. Lewis' line) who need to be built up, and this is often effectively done by reminding ourselves of the commitments that we have made. That's where the disciplines of faith come in and prove themselves so valuable. Such as:

- ◆ Prayer: having conversations with God reminds me of Who is in charge, and who is not. Who is capable of doing the impossible, and who is not.
- ◆ The Word: reading the Bible and allowing its truth and power to wash over me has proven more than just helpful to me—it has literally saved me!
- ◆ Worship: singing out loud (this is only one of many "worship" expressions) builds me up. It is especially impacting when done in community, like on a Sunday morning in church.

APPLICATION▶   Psalm 11 has more than one line, though! To complete the flow of thought, and to build our faith, a few verses later, as if to assuage our need for "evidence", the psalmist provides some points regarding the character of God. In short order he lists:

◆ He still rules (v4a)—this is pure comfort!
◆ He watches everyone closely (v4b)—nothing escapes His notice.
◆ He examines both the righteous and the wicked (v5)—to people who crave "fairness", this is mightily reassuring. I see this as one of the countless acts of kindness the Lord showers His children with. Even though He is not on trial and has no need to defend Himself, He nevertheless graciously says, in effect: "I know you struggle with trusting me sometimes; because I love you so much, let me help you by reminding you of a few more reasons why you can trust Me…"

PRAYER▶

Lord, I trust You. Or maybe more accurately, I want to trust You. I really, really do want to. I admit that I struggle with it sometimes. In Your kindness, can You please help and remind me? Thanks. Amen. So be it.

SEVEN

OUR PROMISE KEEPER

SCRIPTURE ▶ Read Psalm 12.

OBSERVATION ▶ King David frequently did a brilliant job of utilizing contrast to make his point. This psalm is a good example of that. This is a good thing, because in instances in which he begins with a negative perspective, it can look pretty discouraging pretty fast. Make sure that you don't stop after the first 4 verses!

After listing the potentially damaging power of speech— lying, flattery, boastfulness and deception among the negatives—he finally settles in on a singular truth that flies directly in the face of all that junk, and provides stability, hope and direction. It's there that we want to pause and reflect. Verse 6 says this: "The Lord's promises are pure, like silver refined in a furnace, purified seven times over." I see several takeaways in that one short verse. First, it gives us a general clarity of direction, and in this day and age when so many voices cry out and demand attention, that's a very good thing. So, however you choose to go about listening to the Lord, keep at it, for we have the assurance that His voice is pure and true; it is always a solid endeavour and a wise investment!

Secondly, it introduces us to the concept of 'promises'. Now, I've been around long enough to have seen misinterpretations and misuse of God's promises. I've probably misapplied a few myself from time to time! These are usually well intentioned and intended to build faith, or to assist someone on their journey, usually at some difficult or critical moment. Knowing this, I think it's still important to forge ahead with a sense of faith, based on a growing trust in the One who made the promise. In His time, and in His way, He'll instruct you on how to apply the Word, how tightly or loosely to hold on to it, and even provide mature folks around you to help with things like perspective, timing and application. This I know: His promises are pure! Finally, I like the imagery of the purifying process of the furnace. Seven times, the Word says have the promises been run through the fires of purification. To me, that speaks of an added degree of trustworthiness (as if the Lord actually needed that!); in other words, we can trust His promises. Countless saints before us have put those promises to the test, and they have been proven faithful. He will do the same for us!

APPLICATION ▶ If I may, can I offer a couple of things that I have learned through the years about the Lord's promises? (This is by no means comprehensive, nor do I consider it "the last word" on such things. It's just a few things I have discovered along the way.)

- ◆ Be cautious when you apply time frames to His promises. Almost without fail, the mistakes I have made have had to do with misinterpreting timing. Hold promises both firmly and loosely, if that makes sense!

◆ Be careful with whom you share these precious words. Not everyone will understand, and not everyone needs to know. Sometimes they are best held in your heart, for only you and the Lord to process.

◆ Make sure that the promises come from the Word; even prophetic words must submit to the authority of the Bible.

◆ Finally, never stop believing that God loves to speak words of promise and encouragement to His children—that's us!

PRAYER

Lord, I thank you that You are a God who not only makes promises, but also keeps them! Open my heart to hear from You. I trust You to speak in a kind and timely manner.

Bless you, dear listeners...

EIGHT

BLAMELESS

SCRIPTURE ▶ Read Psalm 15.

OBSERVATION ▶ Whenever I read this particular psalm, I'm immediately struck with two distinct, yet profound spiritual truths. These two realities are at the core of the New Covenant, and are the guideposts for effective Christian living. The first truth, and it is front and centre throughout this passage, is: living to please God (this passage actually goes so far as to call it "blameless" (v2)). This is really, really difficult. Okay, let's be honest, it's impossible! It was made manageable back when this was written by the steady stream of sacrificial offerings that were given for 'blame' was transferred to an animal that paid the ultimate price by shedding its blood and dying in the place of the one offering the sacrifice. Regularly carrying out this grisly, but critical requirement ensured that worship of a perfect, holy God could safely take place. By doing so, the invitation to enter into worship in God's presence could be accepted. "Who may worship in Your sanctuary, Lord? Who may enter Your presence on Your holy hill?" (v1)

As if to highlight the difficulty of meeting the qualifications of worshipping this holy God, the rest of the chapter basically lists subsections of the initial requirement: doing what is right and speaking truth (v2), refusing to gossip or speak evil of others (v3), rejecting people who do evil, always keeping one's promises (v4), always dealing with honesty and integrity, and not being tempted to lie (v5). While most would agree that these are all virtuous ideals, the challenge lay in their demanding and comprehensive scope. Jesus clarified their impossibility when He later explained: "You have heard that our ancestors were told, 'you must not murder. If you commit murder, you are subject to judgement.' But I say, if you are even angry with someone, you are subject to judgement." (You can read the entire teaching in Matthew 5) Read that again slowly. You mean, even just getting angry with someone (like, say, in traffic?) has me already guilty, no longer 'blameless'? Which means (according to Psalm 15:1&2) that I'm not actually able to enter God's presence to worship? To echo the hopelessness of the ages, I give you this from the book of Romans, which details this eternal conundrum: "I love God's law with all my heart. (Which is why I long to worship!) But there is another power within me that is at war with my mind (remember Jesus' words about getting angry…). This power makes me a slave to the sin that is still within me (how can I ever be blameless?). "Oh, what a miserable person I am! Who will free me from this life that is dominated by sin and death?" (Romans 7:22-24) That introduces us to the second spiritual reality that I had mentioned off the top: "Thank God! The answer is in Jesus Christ our Lord." (Romans 7:25a) In a nutshell, that is the New Covenant. Jesus takes the 'blame', via His death on the cross, allowing us to answer the question, once and for all, with no fear of retribution, no anxiety regarding our suitability, condition or position in life: "Who can worship, who can enter Your presence?" We can!

APPLICATION ▶ At this point, it's really only a matter of ensuring that one simple step takes place: personalizing the transferring of the blame. Jesus has already taken the blame, and offers this exchange as a gift to us. It only has to be received. If you've never received that offer, now would be a great time to pray (there's a small prayer to guide you included at the back of this book). If you have already received that offer, now would be a great time to praise.

_____

_____

_____

_____

_____

_____

_____

_____

PRAYER

Lord, thank You that You took the blame, therefore, making us blameless before you. I receive this gift (again). Because of this, I happily respond to the invitation to worship! All because of You.

_____

_____

_____

_____

_____

_____

NINE

GOD MY SHELTER

SCRIPTURE Read Psalm 16.

OBSERVATION The other day, I ran out of the medication I take to help keep my blood pressure in check; this probably sounds like something an old person would say, but I was positive that I had more in the medicine cabinet! Anyway, the soonest I could get in to see our doctor was a couple of days away, so I just waited until the appointment, where he took my readings and suggested that if the readings got much higher I should head straight to the hospital! Needless to say, I got the prescription filled and all is fine again in blood pressure land. The reason I tell you that is to highlight a spiritual principle regarding something as simple as what we're doing right now: taking a few moments to spend with the Lord in the Word; in other words, doing our 'devotions'. My little health scare was directly attributable to neglect; nothing more. I had grown a bit casual in my approach to the very serious, potentially life-altering condition that I have and the need to consistently monitor it. It's a little like that with time spent in God's Word. If I'm being completely honest with you, it's a rare occasion in my life when I open my Bible and I experience some sort of huge revelation (you know, lights flashing, angel choirs, words leaping off the page kind of thing!). Mostly, I open my Bible and spend a bit of time quietly reading and mostly pondering. On a practical note, I try to do this early in the morning, immediately after I take my blood pressure medication, (he says sheepishly) in a quiet place, with a Bible that I am familiar with, and usually loosely following some sort of reading plan. That's about it. Nothing fancy, just dutifully taking the prescription. The key is the consistent application (just like medication). Pretty much every day, with very few exceptions, and if not first thing in my day, then almost certainly at another time that day. Missing a few days can sneak up on you and begin to manifest with some real spiritual consequences. The results are not necessarily spectacular in the short term; over the long haul, however, this simple discipline has produced stability in a volatile world, confidence in my inner identity, direction for my life and ministry, rest in a restless world, and comfort in times of crisis, among many other things. Again, the key is showing up regularly, and for me, expectantly. I expect to read, hear, feel or see something from God that will benefit me. Now, enough talking about it, let us go to the Word!

_____

_____

_____

_____

_____

_____

APPLICATION Psalm 16 is one of what I call a "desert island" passage. If you were stranded alone on a desert island, and only had one chapter of the Bible with you to read, Psalm 16 would serve you very well! Rather than highlighting one verse or thought in the midst of a chapter, as I sometimes do, to me, this passage reads best as a whole, one glorious truth following the next. As I was reading this I had this thought: one could simply read one verse a day (yes, only one verse!), meditate on it, regularly returning to it and repeating it, and that would provide a magnificent 11 day devotional). I've never seen Bible reading as a question of quantity, as a competition of any sort, as a checklist to be completed (okay, maybe a bit when I was younger!). Think about it: one verse a day, held closely, pondered deeply and prayerfully, has the potential power to change a life. You could grab a pencil and paper and create a list, if you like. For starters, He keeps me safe (v1); both spoken as a prayer, and as a faith-building reality. He provides me with refuge (v1); He provides me with a sense of direction and action, which I find super helpful. The better I know Him, especially via the Word, the more convinced I am of the security and trustworthiness of Him as a safe place of refuge for my soul. And that's just verse 1! I am going to leave it with you to carry on from here…

PRAYER

Lord, thank You for Your Word. Teach me to desire it. Assist me as I open my Bible, to understand, to apply. Help me to sense Your love of relationship and friendship with me. Grant me a soft heart and a listening ear. Amen.

Carry on, dear friends…

TEN

TRIUMPH OVER MY ENEMIES

SCRIPTURE ▶   Read Psalm 18.

OBSERVATION ▶   I'd like to take a moment to share a very personal story, taken from a couple of verses in the midst of a very long chapter; it was literally a moment that resulted in an expression (one could say an explosion) of faith that changed the course of my life and the depth of my belief. Some might describe it as a prophetic act, or an instance in which I felt that God was speaking directly to me through His Word, and that somehow it required a response. In this instance, I was compelled to act in accordance with my faith.

Let me explain: It was January 2, 2014, to be precise: I know this because I have it dated in the margin of my Bible, right next to the verses that so deeply impacted me (and were later fulfilled as God had said.) The day was cold and overcast as would be expected in January in the part of the world that we live. I was in the regular habit of getting away by myself to quiet, usually scenic locations, which incidentally, is easier in January than in the middle of summer, and this particular day found me at a completely deserted, mostly rocky beach. I set up my folding chair, huddled under a big blanket, and opened my Bible. Before I tell you what I read that day, I will give you a little more. It's no big secret that one of our kids got caught up in a lifestyle that found him addicted to drugs. I'm not talking flirting around the edges with recreational use of soft drugs—we're talking full blown opioid addiction, with all the nastiness that that implies.

The year 2014 was smack in the middle of some of the worst of it, a time that found all of our family grieving deeply and in much pain. That overwhelming sense of a mix sorrow, fear, anger and despair were pretty much a constant in those days. Through it all, each of us tried to navigate the difficulties of our family journey, in our own ways, with varying degrees of faith, sometimes with hope and optimism, oftentimes not. So it was that I opened up my Bible to Psalm 18 and read: "I chased my enemies and caught them; I did not stop until they were conquered. I struck them down so they could not get up; they fell beneath my feet. You have armed me with strength for the battle; you have subdued my enemies under my feet. You placed my foot on their necks" (v37-40). In that moment, a surge of energy pulsed through me: I had a deep inner compulsion and conviction to enact what I was reading. I instinctively knew that I must participate with the Lord in an act of faith that somehow held a key to our family's future and our collective battle with this particular enemy—in our case, drug addiction. And so, I leapt to my feet and began to run down the beach, as though I was pursuing a literal enemy. It was as though, in an act of faith-building and trust, I was declaring for all who might have been watching, seen and unseen: our family will fight by faith, believing that God, and only God, will one day help us to see and experience victory, even though, as I said, these were very bleak days indeed. I ran until I was exhausted; then I found a large boulder and placed my foot upon in it, all the while envisioning this scripture passage being fully and completely true. After a while, now dripping with sweat, I made it back to my lawn chair.

APPLICATION ▶ I realize that each of our faith-journeys is unique. Some may experience visceral moments of faith and trust similar to my story on a regular basis. I do not. This was an individual, personal, and unquestionably profound moment in which something deep inside me was settled. The experience was completed in my heart and spirit well before it was experienced in the flesh (I remind you that start-to-finish, our journey with addiction spanned 10 years of actual addictive behaviours, plus years following of recovery and restoration, for which we are unspeakably grateful). In short, God did what exactly he declared to me on that chilly day way back then. We have partnered and persevered, not always perfectly, but we have seen Him victorious! I suppose how you apply this little example is up to you—I have no real-time instruction for you, no directives to follow. Just a gentle admonition to keep on trusting; and to liberally utilize God's Word in that precious, sometimes precarious process.

PRAYER

I bless you today on your journey. May God bless you through the reading of His Word.

ELEVEN

THE WORD, A SOLID FOUNDATION

SCRIPTURE ▶ Read Psalm 19.

OBSERVATION ▶ Did you ever have an older adult frustrate you in a moment of attempted discipline by saying, "Because I said so!"? It was a response that could drive a young listener crazy, because it signified that any possible bargaining was officially over! Now that I'm a bit older, I understand the dynamics behind that phrase. It's meant to pronounce authority and finality, in other words, the last word of the subject. It is meant to settle the issue, and get down to the business of compliance, and hopefully healthy productivity, at least for the moment! That's kind of how I feel when I read Psalm 19, especially the middle section (not that I opened my Bible this morning looking for an altercation with the Lord!). From verse 7 through to around verse 11, and really to the end of the chapter, the Word makes some declarations about itself; remember, the Word is alive and active (Hebrews 4:12, 2 Timothy 3:16), and so it makes sense that it has the capacity to speak concerning itself, and its work. I once heard a practical piece of advice with regards to approaching the Bible in my devotions, and it has become kind of a lifelong guide: Do you read the Bible, or does the Bible read you? That's the 'alive' part of God's Word. I've lost track of how many times I have opened my Bible, and something has 'spoken' to me, mostly in an inner whisper, but still unmistakably so. Thank God for His Word! So, in regards to the things that the Bible declares about itself, let us do this by listing the verse number, followed by a brief description and comment.

The Word of God:

1. **Instructs**: His instructions are perfect; in other words, they are trustworthy, dependable. The direction they provide have the properties of rejuvenation and refreshing. They provide an inner peace and stability, as well as wisdom when we feel overwhelmed or even foolish.

2. **Commands:** Again, there is a distinct sense of 'rightness' offered to the student of the Word. Unlike a stern, demanding lecturer, however, the Lord's words bring joy! The Word goes on to clarify further that the commands He gives are clear, especially in this age of misinformation and "fake" news. There is no ambiguity here! The result of humbly listening and responding to His commands are insights for daily living. How often through the years have I been the beneficiary of this truth, and in hindsight, how well has this served me!

3. **Is Fair:** Fairness is a massive topic all around us, complete with countless different causes, spoken forcefully by countless different voices. What exactly is fair? While it's unlikely that many of these issues will ever find consensus, the Word makes a sweeping statement about the Lord: He is fair. That's a great relief, and a point of faith to hold on to; no matter what is being said by the world around us, we can ultimately take our cues from the Word.

4. **Is Desirable:** Enough said. Determine to give it access to your inner person—you'll be delighted, and maybe even amazed at how the Word will satisfy you!

5. **Both a warning and a reward:** How helpful and encouraging are both of those concepts? They are simple enough for pretty much anyone to understand: Would it be beneficial to be

warned ahead of potential disaster? Would it be wonderful to know that our gracious and generous God loves to lavish rewards to His Children? I think the simple and obvious answer is: Yes!

APPLICATION   I think that this is a fairly straightforward task: Re-read the passage, note the specific descriptions of the Word, and either: a) remember times that the Lord and His Word have been faithful to do the thing that has been stated, or (b) ask the Lord to deliver the thing He promised in an area of your life that you need it.

PRAYER

Thank you, Lord, for the things Your Word says about itself. I'd love to see and experience each of those attributes and more! Please display the truth of Your Word in every area of my life. Amen. So be it!

Bless you, dear student...

TWELVE

GOD, HAVE YOU ABANDONED ME?

SCRIPTURE ▶ Read Psalm 22.

OBSERVATION ▶ Have you ever seen a familiar face in an unfamiliar setting? It can be a weird experience! We are so accustomed to seeing that face in a recognizable place, perhaps performing a predictable role, and then we are momentarily thrown off in trying to put the encounter into perspective! It happens often to Ingrid and I while we're grocery shopping. The puzzled look on people's faces is priceless. To think that the pastors actually have lives outside the church and pulpit! This Psalm has a component of that, and it starts in the very first verse: "My God, my God, why have You abandoned me?" Can you place where you have heard that before, and who spoke those anguished words? It was Jesus, crying out as He neared the end of His life, while hanging on the cross. (Matthew 27, Mark 15) This is a bit curious, as the psalm is attributed to David. So, what is being communicated here? This psalm contains prophetic words that are mixed in with David's reflections of his own life. Because the Bible is "God-breathed", it has the ability to traverse time, geography, personality and events, to readily settle on any ear willing to listen and respond. So, the Holy Spirit inspired and directed David as he penned these words, a thousand or so years before Jesus lived among mankind on earth, and it is also what gives the Word the ability to speak to us today, another couple of thousand of years later! Further on in the chapter, there are more familiar words concerning Jesus, and they predict specifics surrounding Jesus' ultimate sacrifice for the salvation of all mankind. (Verses 14-18) In my Bible, these verses are all coloured in orange, which is the pencil crayon colour I choose to use any time that the nature and character of Jesus are referenced (there's a colour coding guide at the start of this book, if you'd like to see how I mark my Bible). It's always been like an oasis to me, when I'm reading in the Old Testament, and I spy some orange highlights. I am immediately refreshed as I encounter Jesus, sometimes in quite unlikely places—much like life, wouldn't you say? All that to say, the Word has a beautiful, almost mystical (it's actually more predictable and understandable than it might appear—it's simply the lengths to which God will go to ensure that folks will know, hear, and see His love!) ability to connect to God's heart of love towards us—in this case, through a little glimpse into the future gift His own Son gave for us. It's really a miracle, when you think about it! The rest of the chapter meanders through David's life and looks and feels familiar to any person on any walk of faith. It contains difficult times (v1,2), remembering God's faithfulness in times past (v3-5), a bit of self-loathing despair (v6-8), more declarations of faith and trust (v9,10), desperate prayers (v19-21), the power of praise (v22,23) and more helpful remembrances of God, used to build faith and trust.

APPLICATION ▶ So what to do with a passage such as this? My suggestion, and what I did this morning as I read it, was a slow, thoughtful read, followed by a time of personal communion outside on our front deck. Just me and my Bible, communing with Jesus, thankfully remembering His sacrifice of love for me. An oasis of grace and hope, for sure!

PRAYER

Jesus, thank You for your priceless gift. Help me to remember well the price of love You paid on my behalf. As my life twists and turns, just like King David of old, may I regularly be brought closer to You. Thank You, Lord.

THIRTEEN

THE LORD IS MY SHEPHERD

SCRIPTURE ▶ Read Psalm 23.

OBSERVATION ▶ I've got to admit I feel overwhelmed and inadequate as I view this beloved passage today, preparing to write something for this devotional. I mean, what on earth could anyone possibly compose regarding Psalm 23 that hasn't already been written, and by some of the most brilliant, spiritual and experienced minds at that? And yet, should this humble little devotional collection on Psalms ever land in some unsuspecting reader's hands, would it not appear as the biggest oversight in the history of biblical literature to skip over it? And so, I will pick up my pen and paper, and go where fools fear to tread! As with most of my devotional compositions, this will consist of my personal experience with this passage; how it has embedded and enmeshed itself into my life and ministry, and how I have witnessed the first-hand impact on the lives of others around me. First off, I believe that I have a particularly close identification with it, due to my life assignment as a pastor. Now, most of you know that the best rendering of the word 'pastor' is most likely the word 'shepherd', a word increasingly distant from the life and view of most modern suburbanites. Nevertheless, those were the origins of the author, David the King; the unglamorous, gritty, isolated existence of one who lives alone looking after sheep. And what followed in the psalm were simply lifetime lessons that he learned on the hills in the countryside, before he entered the royal palace with all its privileges and all its treachery. These were lessons that he readily and naturally returned to for the rest of his life. As both a fellow shepherd (in my case, of the people that the Lord has led to the church), and as a fellow pursuer of God (David was known for his zeal to be in close relationship with God), I actually find myself better acquainted with this passage than I have often thought, and I suppose, thus emboldened to plunge ahead writing. As I think about it, perhaps this chapter is best approached via 'Application', so let's briefly apply a bit of its rich content together.

APPLICATION

Verse 1: Pause and imagine the imagery of sheep and shepherds. (Remember, Jesus is the Shepherd, we are the sheep!) Those white puff-balls on the hillside, munching on lush grass have everything they need. Whisper a "thank you" to the Lord!

Verse 2 speaks of rest, nourishment, and the peace that is associated with the Lord's guidance. I'm writing this in the midst of a sabbatical break, so I'm presently experiencing much rest; however, that's not always the case in our lives, is it? Nonetheless, the Shepherd provides rest and guidance—listen and watch for His kind voice.

Verse 3: 'He renews my strength'. I can certainly identify with this truth! Many have been the times when I have wearily wanted to pack it in and He has faithfully shown up in my life to provide endurance, strength and even joy along the way. Ask Him for that promised portion in your life today!

Verse 4&5: As a pastor, this is my go-to passage for the funerals I have been honoured to officiate. I've watched the heavenly mystery of comfort being applied by the tender hand of Jesus, to believers and non-believers alike, based on the true heart of God manifest in this little description. Though we can often feel completely overwhelmed and utterly distracted by moments of grief and pain, may I gently remind you, the Great Shepherd is still there. Look up and look for Him. He's closer than you think, and His desire and joy is to bless you with love and kindness.

Verse 6: How often I have come to this conclusion and been blessed and encouraged by it: While I thought I was the one pursuing God, I actually had it backwards—HE pursues ME, with goodness and unfailing love! Even in times when I imagined myself to be running away from Him, He doggedly wouldn't give up on me. Finally, an eternal promise to finish the chapter—no wonder it's probably the best known chunk of the entire Bible!

PRAYER

Take any one of the little snippets mentioned in any one of the verses above and speak it as a simple request—they'll all suffice just fine! Bless you, fellow sheep...

FOURTEEN
GOD, I TRUST IN YOU

SCRIPTURE ▶ Read Psalm 25.

OBSERVATION ▶ I'd like to take a look at the "book ends" of this psalm today; there is plenty of outstanding, impacting content in the middle, to be sure (words of encouragement, hints on receiving direction, gentle instruction, notes on the character of God), but for our purposes, basically just the first and last thoughts will occupy this particular devotional. For me, these two statements really comprise the essence of the journey of faith as a born-again believer; they are declarations that are most likely made at the beginning of the faith-journey, are regularly repeated throughout that journey and are the basis of trust and hope as life on earth comes to a close. I have often thought that if you only had these two verses in the entire Bible to guide your worship and understanding of God, and to contemplate and meditate upon for the span of your life, they would be more than enough! Curious? Let's have a look then and make some practical application.

Verse 1 describes the divine exchange that takes place at the beginning of our journey of faith; and it quickly follows with the lifelong prescription that will be necessary to apply and re-apply for the rest of our days:"O Lord, I give my life to You. I trust in You, my God". Such simple concepts, and yet so profoundly difficult to do! I suppose the challenge lies in the oh-so-human tendency to renege on the commitment that we're making when we hand over our lives to God. Age and maturity play a role here, because if we make the choice to give our lives to God (for our purposes here, we'll call that a "salvation" experience) when we are young, we really have no clue about the challenges this will present down the road; it was simply a genuine and natural exchange, probably very easy as well. If we were older at the time of that choice, we are already more adept at the art of negotiation, and that can prove both troublesome and exhausting, as we invariably work out the practice and nuance of faith. How many times have I found myself re-giving, re-dedicating or re-committing myself to God, simply because at some point, I found myself desperately trying to take back control of my life and circumstances? This doesn't make me a bad Christian, it makes me human! It generally looks like this: when things are going well in my life, I'm content with the exchange: God appears to be doing His part by making me happy, so the arrangement apparently works. Then, trouble comes, as it does for everyone, I begin to question the decision I've made to "give my life to Him." Surely, I could do a better job at producing a happy life, so I "take back" control of my life. Do you recognize this? This quickly (or sometimes not so quickly) reveals itself as a mistake, as I am fundamentally unable to control and manage the complexities of my life, let alone the lives of others. Hopefully, I return to the conclusion that the only and best way to proceed is through trust: "I trust in You, my God."

Now, to the other "bookend", in conclusion, and this is possibly best contained via "Application".

APPLICATION   "...I put my hope in You" (21b) It all sounds so good, so easy, doesn't it? In truth, it actually is. It is nothing more complicated than that—learning to trust. There is an inevitability about having to learn to trust in the Christian life. Trust will be ultimately verified because of the One in whom we are placing our confidence in, God Himself! Over time, after much repetition and much failure, we are learning to trust God to the point where trust morphs into something even greater: hope. Hope is not in the circumstances, but rather in the unshakable character of Father God. How do we go about developing and nurturing this hope and trust? There are many ways, I suppose, but none as straightforward as the two things we're doing today: reading the Word and prayer.

PRAYER

Lord, I give my life to you again...and again...Teach me to trust again...and again...Help me to experience hope again...and again...So be it.

FIFTEEN
GOD'S TESTING

SCRIPTURE Read Psalm 26.

OBSERVATION This psalm contains a concept that I have always found to be very intriguing. Additionally, I have found it to be true in my own life. The concept has to do with one of the many expressions of the character and nature of God: He is a 'tester'. It shows up in verse 2: "Put me on trial, Lord, and cross-examine me. Test my motives and my heart." The idea of God 'testing' is it not new; the reason it stands out to me is that I have seen it elsewhere in the Bible, enough times to note a commonality in God's dealing with people.

For example:

- ◆ God tested Abraham (Genesis 22:1)
- ◆ God tested an entire people group (Judges 2:21,22)
- ◆ King David stated as much (Psalm 17:3), and actually invited the process (Psalm 139:23)
- ◆ Proverbs uses it as a life illustration (17:3)
- ◆ James lists it as an expected part of the life of faith (James 1:3)

Okay, so we've determined that God partners with us through the reality of 'tests' that show up in our lives. I think that probably needs a bit of clarification, and maybe I'll start with what it is not, because there will almost certainly be opportunities to misinterpret this concept and the degrees and intentions of God's involvement in the process.

Let's begin with the heart of God, with regards to testing. He is completely and utterly kind; so let's remove from our thinking any picture or belief of an angry, cruel taskmaster, someone who uses testing in order to punish, ridicule or demean. That is the furthest thing from the truth. It is, however, a critical understanding as we develop this thought—any misunderstanding could easily lead to a very skewed view of God, one that is constantly suspicious of His participation in our lives, which is extremely detrimental to fostering a growing, trusting relationship with our Heavenly Father. Here's how I have come to understand the testing and the Tester, and it mostly comes down to 3 things: God's character, God's intentions, and God's methods, and they all of stack upon each other, like building blocks. Briefly, here's how it works: If God is utterly, completely and perfectly kind (that's building block #1, the foundation), then we can trust and believe that His intentions towards us are always and only good (that's building block #2). Therefore, when difficult things happen in our lives, which is of course common to everyone, we can rest in the knowledge that it is highly unlikely that He caused the painful, hurtful occurrence, but His methods indicate that He will lovingly partner with us (building block #3) in the deepening and formation of the most precious commodity in the life of a follower of God: faith.

APPLICATION ▶ I realize that this little lesson could become a very big, cumbersome, even troublesome lesson very quickly. I don't mean to minimize anyone's pain or dismiss the hard and unfair things of life. I really believe (and my life's experience has shown this to be true) that a faith-filled grasp of this concept can be helpful, useful and downright life-giving! How then, to apply? For me, it's always started with slowing things down, pausing amidst the turmoil and emotion of the moment, and returning to that first little building block: God is always and only kind and loving towards me. I would encourage you to do the same.

As my Mom used to always say: "This too, shall pass". She also always said: "The key to life in Christ? Trust, trust, trust." I believe that she was correct, on both accounts.

PRAYER ▶

I'm going to go for a walk now. While I'm out walking, I'm going to review today's Application, and phrase it as a prayer. I hope you'll join me in doing the same.

SIXTEEN
I LONG TO BE WITH GOD

SCRIPTURE ▸   Read Psalm 26.

OBSERVATION ▸   As is common to anyone who has ever found themselves falling in love, I was giddy with excitement every time I was going to see my girlfriend, Ingrid, who happily later became my wife. I recall one particular occasion before we were married, when she and her family had left town for a couple of days, not far, just to a small lakefront resort town fairly close by. We were only going to be apart for a weekend, but it seemed like an aching eternity to me! So, I hatched a plan to drive out after work one evening to where they were, a distance of about 100 kilometres, just to see her for a moment, just to hear her voice and hand her a cheap bouquet of corner store flowers. This was in the days before cell phones, so my surprise arrival was all part of the excitement! It might sound a bit anticlimactic, but that's the extent of the story. Nothing funny or foolish happened; there were no accidents on the highway, I didn't get lost on the way, her family didn't seem particularly annoyed that I briefly barged in on their time away. The entirety of that little story is captured by this thought: I longed to be with her. No distance, no cost, no inconvenience, no time would keep me from coming to her. Ten minutes with her was enough to temporarily satisfy me, and afterwards I just drove straight back home with a foolish grin on my face—it had been worth it! (I probably would have driven out the next evening as well, but for the look that her Dad gave me as I climbed back into my car for the trip home!)

I was reminded of that moment this morning when I read Psalm 27, especially verse 8: "My heart has heard you say, "Come and talk with me." And my heart responds, "Lord, I am coming." Of all the things that the Lord has generously given me, and the list is extensive, perhaps the thing that I am most thankful for is this: a responsive heart. I don't say that with any sense of pride; it is only and completely from Him. Why He chose to do this is sometimes still puzzling to me, though, as I said, I am eternally grateful. Ever since I was a little boy, I have had a desire to know about God, and more importantly, to know Him. That desire has guided me through the wilful foolishness of my teenage years, and through a period in which I purposefully ran away from the sense of calling that God was whispering over my life. In the face of numerous inconsistencies and a string of poor choices, there remained in me a constant, deep down, longing to be close to God. I don't pull the "ancient language" card very often, but I think it works really well in this instance. The Greek rendering of the word 'heard' (or 'listen') in this verse is Akoua: to listen with the heart. Of all the things I have read in the Word about developing a close relationship with the Lord, that comes closest to explaining it: having and maintaining a soft, listening heart.

APPLICATION ▶   I know that for some, this is a somewhat mystifying concept, conceivably something so vague that it may appear impossible to experience. As I said earlier, it's always been intuitive to me, natural in virtually every way, which could make it even more frustrating for some. I recognize that, I really do. However, the importance of learning to listen, hear and respond is so valuable that I'm unwilling to let it go as simply a 'wiring' thing: in other words, you're either born with the inclination or you're not. To my way of thinking, there must be ways to nurture and develop this precious ability, and I believe there is. If I could give some simple insight in to you, this is what I'd say: Determine deep down, in your inner person, that you desire to be close to the Lord, that you really long to listen and hear His voice. After all, He says that He will grant the desires of our hearts (Psalm 37:4), the desires that truly honour Him, and certainly, that must be at the top of the list!

PRAYER ▶

Pause for a moment and form a prayer that expresses, however clumsily it might come out, your desire to be close and responsive to the Lord. My heart has heard you say, "Come and talk with me". And my heart responds, "Lord, I am coming." As for me, I'm going for a walk and talk in the stillness of the early morning. Bless you, dear listeners...

SEVENTEEN

MAJESTIC GOD!

SCRIPTURE ▶ Read Psalm 29.

OBSERVATION ▶ I bumped into an interesting contrast today, as I read Psalm 29. Yesterday's devotional was very much still on my mind (the one about responsive hearts and quiet, inner listening from Psalm 27) when this passage barged into my life, with all its imagery of shouting and thunder and loudness. What's a lover of the "gentle whisper" (often referred to as the "still, small voice" 1 Kings 19:12) to do?

Simply put, God cannot be simply defined in narrow, constricted terms. Because of who He is, and His unlimited nature, it is a mistake to assume that He can only be approached or worshipped in one way. Now, we as humans tend to really like familiarity and predictability, especially when it comes to things that are somewhat mystical and unseen, much like the act of worship. So, we begin to fall into a recognizable 'groove' when it comes to the worship of God; certain songs, styles, methods, volumes, particular settings or locations give us great comfort and make it feel more conducive to worship. In fact, the presence of these things often determine the quality, depth and duration of our encounters with the Lord. Their absence can even make it very difficult (sadly, in some cases, impossible) to enter into God's presence and into a worshipful state. For me, maybe that's the point of this rather jarring psalm; as much as I easily and naturally experience God in quiet, restful times, His bigness insists that He is equally available to be discovered in power and majesty. As always, it comes down to the quality of listening, the process of awareness that we bring to the table.

APPLICATION ▸   I'm going to try to really embrace this. Rather than write it from a point of instruction to everybody else (I think I'm guilty of this from time to time), I'm going to lift my head up, and really try to look to the bigness of the Lord. It's funny, come to think of it, and I just thought of this: when I walk into a forest, for example, I naturally tend to look down, looking for tiny things, things that aren't readily or obviously visible— I've always done this. It's a habit. Here's about the most practical application I can imagine for myself: I'm literally going to the forest today and looking up! Or to the ocean and looking out! Or to the skies and looking beyond! "The voice of the Lord echoes above the sea. The glory of God thunders. The Lord thunders over the mighty sea. The voice of the Lord is powerful; the voice of the Lord is majestic. The voice of the Lord splits the mighty cedars; The Lord shatters the cedars of Lebanon. The voice of the Lord strikes with bolts of lightning. The voice of the Lord makes the barren wilderness quake; The Lord shakes the wilderness of Kadesh. The voice of the Lord twists mighty oaks and strips the forest bare. In His Temple everyone shouts "Glory!" (29: 3-5, 7-9)

PRAYER

Lord, overwhelm me today with Your majesty; Impress upon my tiny heart Your glory; please give me a glimpse into Your greatness! Help me to cry out "Glory!" To the forest I go! Bless you, dear friends, in the big and the small...

EIGHTEEN

GOD'S CONSTANT FAITHFULNESS

SCRIPTURE   Read Psalm 30.

OBSERVATION   The introductory heading in my Bible states that this psalm was written by David, as a song in anticipation of the dedication of the Temple. (I don't usually use introductory headings as the basis for teaching, but I think you'll get the point!) Conceivably, this would be an absolute high point in his life, a time for great praise and thankfulness, a moment of joyous celebration. It would also be a time to reflect on the difficulties and challenges that had been faced and overcome along the way, and, of course, God's faithfulness and provision. He was wise and humble enough to know that without the Lord's Hand of strength and guidance, the big day of celebration simply would never materialize. (As an aside, I recognize the rush of emotion that he expressed, having had the honour of pastoring a church through a building program a few years back, with all its ups and downs, culminating in a somewhat similar, though less ostentatious, moment of genuine celebration.)

History, however, allows us a unique opportunity to view the story in context, and ultimately this helps us process our own lives and faith. What I mean is this: we can read David's story before the big dedication day ever arrives and we can also read about his life well afterwards. In both cases, there were many instances of trial, pain and confusion, and moments of utter despair. Verses 1-3 indicate as much, and verse 5 articulates the flow of life like this: "Weeping may last through the night, but joy comes with morning." That's faith and hope in action, isn't it? And so, across the span of our lives, there will be moments of great, sometimes giddy joy and rightful celebration; there will also be times when things get really hard, sometimes very quickly, and sometimes for a very long time. When the king composed this psalm, he had no idea of the bitter, painful experiences that lay ahead of him, he only had hindsight regarding God's faithfulness and patience, and the joy of God's presence and activity in his life right then. For example, we know that he himself never actually got to see the day of dedication, it fell to his son Solomon to build and finally dedicate the Temple. (1 Kings 8) So, in effect, he wrote this celebratory passage, because he knew in his heart of hearts that God had asked him to partner in the building of the long-awaited Temple. He did it out of obedience and faith, not knowing when or if he would actually be there on the grand day of dedication. He penned these words, and in faith he would celebrate and honour God; across his life, he had certainly seen God faithfully active to this point, and he would use those understandings and experiences to forge ahead in faith, intent on serving and honouring the Lord, no matter what lay ahead. Sound familiar? It's really the blueprint for our lives, isn't it?

APPLICATION ▶ For me, the last 3 verses say it best, and reflect the hope we all carry: "Hear me, Lord, and have mercy on me. Help me, O Lord. You have turned my mourning into joyful dancing. You have taken away my clothes of mourning and clothed me with joy, that I might sing praises to You and not be silent. O Lord my God, I will give you thanks forever." (Psalm 30: 10-12)

PRAYER

This is pretty simple, because it reflects our faith-journeys so well: Read those three verses as a prayer; with growing faith and trust, remembering God's faithfulness in the past, enjoying His blessings in the present, and hoping in His Goodness for the future. Just like a king did a couple of thousand years earlier!

NINETEEN

REPENTANCE & FORGIVENESS, GOD'S GIFT

SCRIPTURE ▸   Read Psalm 32.

OBSERVATION ▸   We watched a kids cartoon with our grandson the other day; it's a show that we all like. It's about a family of cats, there are three siblings, and they purport to show life and some of the lessons that cat families discover and learn. In this particular seven-minute episode, one of the cat children (kittens, I guess) eats a cake that has been set aside for the entire family to enjoy later, and then creates a wild story to cover it up (we used to call that "lying"). The fraud is soon discovered, and the result is that the young cat must bake another cake, with the help of the Dad cat, who happens to be an excellent baker. Then they all happily eat the new cake together, the narrator intoning that it's best to tell the truth—the end.

Ingrid and I looked at each other and wondered aloud: "Cute story, but where was the consequence of lying, of deceiving the family?" There was no "I'm sorry", no "please forgive me", "I'll try not to do that again"...there was just...more cake. Now, I'm not advocating for corporal cat punishment; nor am I suggesting something along the lines of harsh discipline and angry words of condemnation. We were just left wondering if something was ultimately missing. I was reminded of that when I read Psalm 32 this morning. The topic of forgiveness and repentance are mentioned several times throughout the passage, including the very first couple of verses, which seemed to jump off the page to me: "Oh, what joy for those whose disobedience is forgiven, whose sin is put out of sight! Yes, what joy for those whose record the Lord has cleared of guilt…" (v 1&2a) While not terribly popular, oftentimes studiously omitted, or even considered to be irrelevant by some, there remains an eternal truth at play in the lives of every human being (okay, every cartoon cat family, too!): the concepts of sin, repentance and forgiveness. These could quite easily be described as the core of Christian belief, because providing sufficient answers to all of these conundrums runs straight through the centre of the life, death and resurrection of Jesus, the founder of our faith and the object of our belief. Another point of note in my Bible: I regularly mention my practice of colour-coding verses that stand out to me. (Go to the opening pages of this book if you'd like further details on how I go about this) Psalm 32 begins with a couple of colours, the most prominent being orange, the pencil crayon I use to highlight anything about Jesus. So, in the middle of Psalms, written many hundreds of years before Jesus came onto the scene in the flesh, He prominently appears with a glimpse into what His life and death would mean: the way to forgiveness, guilt-free living and true inner freedom! The central importance of this reality is repeated again a few verses later: "Finally, I confessed all my sins to you and stopped trying to hide my guilt (how our cat family needed to understand this!).I said to myself, "I will confess my rebellion to the Lord." And You (orange pencil crayon) forgave me! All my guilt is gone!" (v5)

APPLICATION ▶ Even more remarkable is the knowledge and perspective that we are granted, due to us living in the present and available grace of the New Covenant. Remember, David wrote this well before Jesus' time and ultimate sacrifice on earth—his experience of forgiveness and the removal of guilt would have only come via the regular sacrifice of animals and the shedding of their blood. How understandably limited his view was at the time! And here's where literal 'application' comes in: we have the astonishing, privileged ability to live guilt-free, and to experience the lightness and joy of living that way. The only qualifiers are repentance and acceptance by faith, the thing that I would humbly suggest our little cat family missed.

PRAYER ▶

I heartily encourage us all to do a quick review of our lives, with an eye to confession and repentance. For our little cat friend, it might sound something like this: "Heavenly Father, I confess to You that I lied to my family, and then I covered up that lie. I repent of that sin. I'm truly sorry for doing that. Thank You that You will forgive me because Jesus has taken my guilt away when He died to pay for the consequences of my lie. I receive that forgiveness by faith, and I ask You to help me get better at telling the truth". This is an exercise that should never get old, nor should it be unfamiliar to us as believers. As I've often said, why waste another moment feeling distant from God, when the road has been paved for us to walk in closeness!...Bless you, dear friends...

TWENTY

GOD'S GRAND PERSPECTIVE

SCRIPTURE ▸   Read Psalm 33.

OBSERVATION ▸   It's hard to know where to start with this psalm. There's just so much in it, and there's so many different directions that one could take! For example, the first couple of verses are really a call to praise; an invitation to worship (v1-3). It is a Sunday morning as I read this portion of scripture and I can almost feel myself being pulled up from my recliner and drawn to the house of the Lord! Even if I didn't make it to church, or if it wasn't a Sunday, the urging is clear: bring a joyful offering of praise to the Lord today, for it's the good and right thing to do! Slipped in next is a quick reminder of the importance and trustworthiness of the Word "For the word of the Lord holds true, and we can trust everything He does." (v4) Simple and to the point. Pretty self-explanatory! Lord, help this become a reality in my life. This is followed by a few verses that illuminate the character and nature of God (highlighted in yellow in my Bible). I just love seeing these magnificent descriptors of my Heavenly Father. They build my faith and confidence in Him; they deepen my capacity to trust. When I find myself in a complicated, difficult circumstance, a quick read of something like this provides me with hope and strength—after all, if God is big enough to speak the heavens into existence (v6), surely, He's big enough to handle my situation, right? The lens widens over the next couple of verses (v13-17), almost as though God is pulling back the curtains and inviting us in to see something truly remarkable, a glimpse into God's very own perspective. Any time I see something like this in scripture; it captivates me on a different level. I mean, think about it; seeing something (people, crisis, world situations) through God's perspective is a truly amazing thing! Take a moment to close your eyes and let your imagination paint this awesome picture for you. Not only does He see the whole human race, verse 15 tells us He understands every detail, every motivation, every innermost thought. Astonishing and comforting in the same breath! Verse 16 begins a two-verse transition where that lens begins to narrow again—from the big, broad picture of the whole of humanity at once, to a comforting vision of the individual care and attention that He gives to each of His children. The psalmist eases us into the transition by directing our thoughts and hearts to the only safe place to be; not in kings or warriors, armies or nations, but safely and contentedly in Him. What gentle yet powerful hope arises with the truth of verse 18: "...the Lord watches over those who fear Him, those who rely on His unfailing love." A quick reminder, though you've most likely heard this many times before, the 'fear' referenced in this verse is not what almost immediately springs to mind: terror, uncertainty, dread. It is a healthy, thoughtful, reasoned reverence and respect of God, based on the strength of relationship with Him, built and proven trustworthy over the years by loving interaction with Him. Big difference. Finally, another call to action (v20-22). To me, this passage is all about building faith. It's a narrative that leads us through the challenges of life, while always gently nudging us toward the safety and security of God's care.

APPLICATION ▶   That's how I process a passage like Psalm 33. What do you think? Perhaps you glean something quite different; regardless, I believe that ultimately this psalm, at its core is about responsiveness to the Lord, which will inevitably build trust in Him. For a literal application, why don't you jot down your own reflections, section by section, as you slowly consider it? I have a sneaking suspicion that Psalm 33 might become a favourite of yours going forward!

PRAYER ▶

"For the word of the Lord holds true, and we can trust everything He does." Lord, open our eyes and hearts to this profound truth. Grow our roots deep in faith. Grow our trust in You. Help us to experience the security of Your unfailing love (v 18). Amen. So be it.

TWENTY-ONE
WORSHIP THE LORD

SCRIPTURE ▶ Read Psalm 34.

OBSERVATION ▶ The first verses of this psalm come flooding back into my memory as I read them today. There was a time in not-too-distant Church history that our song services often came directly from scripture; such was the case of Psalm 34:1-4. I can still remember the tune, too! Throughout this passage there are numerous qualifiers regarding those who are a good fit for worshipping God; they're not necessarily what you might think! (Which, by the way, is really good news for us) How often in my life have I sought to 'disqualify' myself from worship? Too many times to count, for sure! Let me explain in very simple point form what I mean by that:

Intellectually, I know that worshipping the Lord is healthy and good for me, but…

◆ My mind, thoughts, and feelings often rise up and try to prevent me from entering into worship and then receiving the benefits of being close to God, so…

◆ I find myself excusing myself from participating, whether in a church service or on my own…This might sound something like: "I've had a tough week and I don't feel like praising God today", or "I've got too many hard things going on in my life—I can't be expected to focus on God right now", or "I'll feel like a phony, worshipping the Lord when my life is so far from perfect", or maybe "I don't deserve to be in God's presence; I've done some pretty bad stuff recently". Does any of this sound familiar? Let's face it, it's not always the easiest or most natural thing to worship God. The truth is, it's not supposed to be based on ease or fun or feelings. This is actually a good thing, because the offer to worship must be accessible whenever, wherever, and by whoever is wise enough to desire health and wholeness. So, what were the 'qualifiers' for entering into worship that I mentioned off the top? (In addition to this list, it might be helpful to look up David's traumatic story in 1 Samuel 21:10-15 to get a clearer picture of what he was going through)

Does any of this sound familiar? Let's face it, it's not always the easiest or most natural thing to worship God. The truth is, it's not supposed to be based on ease or fun or feelings. This is actually a good thing, because the offer to worship must be accessible whenever, wherever, and by whoever is wise enough to desire health and wholeness. So, what were the 'qualifiers' for entering into worship that I mentioned off the top? (In addition to this list, it might be helpful to look up David's traumatic story in 1 Samuel 21 to get a clearer picture of what he was going through)

- ◆ the helpless (v2)
- ◆ the fearful (v4)
- ◆ the desperate (v6)
- ◆ the troubled (v6)
- ◆ the needy (v9)
- ◆ the troubled (v 17, 19)
- ◆ the broken-hearted (v18)
- ◆ the crushed (v18)
- ◆ the servant (v22)
- ◆ the righteous (v9,15,19,21)

Remember that our 'righteousness' is a gift from the Lord, it is not of our own doing. I don't know about you, but that makes the prospect of worshipping the Lord more approachable for me! In fact, the time to worship is preferably best done when I find myself identified with one of those things on the list. It helps to articulate my need for God; and it helps to prioritize and clarify who is actually my source—God or me! When you think about it for a moment, this is precisely what worship is really all about.

APPLICATION Put aside today's "to-do" list if you can, and purposefully slow things down for a moment. Do whatever you can do to put yourself in a posture and place of worship. Use a favourite worship song. Close your eyes. Breathe a prayer. Read a personally meaningful psalm. Change your position. Look at something beautiful. Ponder God's greatness.

PRAYER

Use any of the above suggestions or compose your own.

"Taste and see that the Lord is good. Oh, the joys of those who take refuge in Him." Amen. So be it.

TWENTY-TWO

DELIGHT YOURSELF IN THE LORD

SCRIPTURE Read Psalm 37.

OBSERVATION Ever since I was a young boy, I've always had a love for the Bible. I likely wouldn't have necessarily been able to articulate it well back then; I just always had a gentle affection for it. I liked its feel in my hands, it's weight in my lap. The thinness of its pages; even the illustrations depicting famous scenes in my very first child's Bible. Okay, especially the illustrations! Regardless, the Bible has always felt like a friend to me.

This psalm contains one of the very first times the Lord began to develop and reveal His plans for me, as He gave me an inkling of the beginnings of becoming a pastor, a shepherd. Again, I would not have recognized it as such, but upon reflection I can clearly still recall the interaction. I'd like to share it with you.

It came by way of noticing (the first time, as far as I can tell) a pattern, a teaching, that could be shown to others as a way of explaining and nurturing a growing relationship with the Lord. I can remember excitedly circling the words in my Bible (this may have also been the first time I ever thought to note something of importance that had caught my attention—a practice that I still regularly do more than 50 years later!), and then recognizing that these could be presented in point form, in the form of preaching or teaching. It was thrilling to me!

Here's what I saw all those years ago. In quick succession, between verses 3 and 7, there are 4 practical things that a person could do to enhance their trust in God. (Of course, to a teenage boy, they all seemed so straightforward, so simple, so easy— while still utterly true, they have proven a tad more challenging in practice). Verse 3 starts with "Trust" as the first building block; as if to re-emphasize the importance of trusting God, it's the only one of the four directives that is repeated (verse 4). In the life of a follower of Jesus, there is probably no point as important. It is the absolute bedrock of belief and understanding; it will be presented to us on a shockingly regular and very personal basis: "Do you trust Me?" Our answer is really the key to our faith-walk. The next point is quick to follow: "Take delight in the Lord". (v4) How often I forget this simple instruction! Did you know it is okay to enjoy your walk with Jesus? That may be the single greatest piece of wisdom that this entire book contains! The next step looks easy on paper, but takes a lot of practice, and frankly, a lot of failure: "Commit everything you do to the Lord." (v5) I'm still working at this, but I'd be happy to sit down to compare notes! I'm convinced, however, that ultimately it is the way to live by faith and trust. Finally, verse 7 gives the age-old advice to "be still", followed by "wait patiently". Those thoughts go hand in hand with each other. In other words, be still and watch patience grow.

APPLICATION ▶ I'm normally not a 'list' maker when it comes to spiritual growth. I tend to find it too formulaic, too forced, too programmed. But I'll make an exception in this case: Read Psalm 37:3-7 again and circle the instructions; ponder their meaning in your own life.

_____

_____

_____

_____

_____

_____

_____

_____

PRAYER ▶

Lord, help me to faithfully do the things I just circled, and to know and experience the fruit and friendship that they promise.

_____

_____

_____

_____

_____

_____

_____

_____

TWENTY-THREE

GOD IS ABSOLUTELY FAITHFUL

SCRIPTURE ▶ Read Psalm 40.

OBSERVATION ▶ This psalm presents itself to me in the form of a checklist of sorts: there's a whole bunch of separate observations on a variety of subjects, each of which I can look at and say with confidence: Yup, I've seen that one in my life! "Check another box of the Lord's faithfulness!" A brief walk through of the psalm kind of looks like this: Verses 1-3 describes the many times the Lord has come to my help; the countless times He has rescued me and "lifted me out of the pit of despair." (v2) I even recognize those moments when a "new song" of praise has erupted from within me. Take a moment to remember your own journey with the Lord—I'm sure you'll see the same thing! The last part of verse 3 brings a great sense of hope and purpose in the face of sometimes confusing circumstances. "Many will see what He has done and be amazed." Lord, may that be the story of our lives! The next couple of verses check the boxes of who God is and what He is like, and by extension, what those magnificent truths bring to my life: "Oh, the joys of those who trust the Lord." (v4) Seen it. Experienced it. Another check mark. Verse 8 gives an indication of how we can approach God; for what we're hoping for as far as fruit and results. "Your instructions are written on my heart." We don't just read the Word as an exercise, we read it to better know its Author. Lord, I give you permission to continue writing in me. Verses 9 and 10 remind us of why going to church is so important. Check. Another cry to the Lord, asking for His unfailing love and faithfulness to surround and protect us. (v11,12,13) Verse 16 brings more hopefulness, and the possibility of salvation and restoration: "...repeatedly shout, "The Lord is great!"" More times than I can count. And in conclusion, a final, humble confession: "As for me, since I am poor and needy, let the Lord keep me in His thoughts. (how truthful and humbling is that?) You are my helper and my saviour. O my God, do not delay."

APPLICATION   Maybe you literally make a checklist and then take some time to remember and recall God's faithfulness. Of this you can be sure: God will not come up short. He will be shown to be absolutely faithful, and that we will never run out of boxes that we can check in describing His goodness and love towards us!

PRAYER

I think we just did...Keep up the good work, dear friends...

TWENTY-FOUR

THE "I WILL" OF FAITH

SCRIPTURE   Read Psalm 42.

OBSERVATION   Have you ever had a day in which you wake up, get ready for the day full of promise and possibilities, when all of a sudden, out of nowhere, something or someone brings you some very difficult news? Well, I just had one of those experiences today; as the shock of the news settles over you, you feel numb and even disbelieving; in my case, I felt like I had run headlong into a brick wall, leaving me dazed and winded! Of course, there are then the inevitable questions directed toward and about God. For me, the questions are not so much about why He would let something happen, or even how He could have prevented things, nor does it raise questions about His character; those questions were settled in my heart long ago. My human response is more about what's next. The greatest faith-obstacle in my world is the great unknown: what on earth are we going to do now?

Psalm 42 reminds me of these things, as I steady myself following the delivery of disappointing, shocking news. In fact, the divisions and emphasis in this passage land more on the difficult realities that the writer is experiencing, and less on solutions and immediate answers, which I find both honest and helpful. It begins with an expression of longing for God's presence (v1,2), a recognition that although things are not right in the world around us, there's still something that instinctively draws us towards God. A longing, even as vague as it might appear, that our best hope is found in Him.

As I read today, I was struck by the intensity of feeling that is being expressed; it is so very real in its depiction of the jumble of thoughts and emotions that we feel in these trying times. The author remembers when things were so much better, and this seems to make the pain even worse! (v4) The writing is like a window into human confusion and pain: we can feel the desperate swinging of emotion and mood, as we are exposed to this hard, hard moment. And then, it's like an inner light bulb of faith goes on suddenly, and before hope is extinguished, it flickers to life again: "Why am I discouraged? Why is my heart so sad?" This is the lightbulb moment: "I will put my hope in God! I will praise Him again—my Saviour and my God!" This inner dialogue pattern is repeated again a few verses later (v11) as the tumult of emotions rages unabated all around. Note that the psalmist's declarations are action based, and that's an important consideration. As tough as it seems and even though it might even feel pointless, faith compels us forward, and expressing that faith is critical, in order to combat a rising sense of hopelessness. "I will" is the key to faith. There is an inner determination to seek closeness with God, no matter how bleak things might appear. "I will put my hope in God!" The passage also contains a helpful little template for making it through another day, a simple model for surviving difficult times, and it's slipped in almost unnoticed in the middle of the chapter: "But each day the Lord puts His unfailing love upon me, and through each night I sing His songs, praying to God who gives me life." (v8) It is disarmingly simple. We repeatedly declare that His love will never run out, and we express that, sometimes in bitter tears, through worship and prayer.

_____

_____

_____

_____

_____

APPLICATION   If you're going through something really tough right now, this psalm could well be a very timely gift to you—it was for me this morning. Maybe you could just take the model we just discussed and simply let it wash over you. Or just quietly re-read the whole psalm and let it become your prayer.

_____

_____

_____

_____

_____

PRAYER

> _I'm glad that we could have this chat, you and I and the Lord._
> _It might not feel like much, but we offer a simple expression of faith_
> _and trust in You, Lord. In the middle of the difficult things of our_
> _lives, may we sense Your unfailing love and grace. Grant us strength_
> _and endurance, Lord. Amen._
>
> _Bless you, dear friends..._

_____

_____

_____

_____

TWENTY-FIVE

LIGHT AND TRUTH FROM GOD

SCRIPTURE ▶ Read Psalm 43.

OBSERVATION ▶ "Send out Your light and Your truth; let them guide me. Let them lead me to Your holy mountain, to the place where You live." (3)

How often in my life have I desperately needed guidance and direction? As I take even a quick glance across my years, I can put together a pretty significant list; choosing a life partner, losing and finding employment, buying houses, parenting children, leading a church…the list goes on. I referenced this again in yesterday's thoughts with the question: What's next? If you're anything like me, this has been a fairly common occurrence, so let's have a closer look at these couple of verses and see what we can discover. This passage contains several useful insights regarding clarifying God's direction, or at least providing some simple steps to take with that in mind. To be honest, finding God's direction (some would call it God's "will") is something that is admittedly challenging on occasion, especially so when there is a crisis involving time and deadlines. It all looks pretty neat and tidy from the relative calm of my recliner with a cup of coffee, right?

I said that the steps were simple, and they really are. Before I go any further, it's important to remember that applying the instructions here is not a guarantee of instant clarity and smooth sailing. Expecting this type of "magic wand" result will inevitably lead to disappointment. Having said that, how then do we go about receiving the comfort and assurance that the Bible says is available? Verse 3 declares that there are two things that God "sends out": light and truth. If we envision the times of our lives when we need clear direction as "dark" and/or "uncertain" moments, then this is immediately encouraging. Light and truth will be of immense help in finding my way; light to show where to step, and truth to ensure that the place that I step is secure. "Let them [light and truth] guide me". The next little exercise is tremendously simple—look at what you're holding in your hands: the Word of God. Psalm 119:105 says it this way: "Your word is a lamp to guide my feet and a light for my path." While I've never really experienced a literal explosion of light to show me the path forward, I have nonetheless been the regular recipient of God's comforting direction, oftentimes in a whisper, frequently when I wasn't really expecting it, but always right on time. I think I could even chronicle times when the Lord, in His infinite patience, has repeatedly pointed out a direction that I was too dense or distracted to pick up! Light and truth are best discovered over time, and regular, familiar, time visiting with the Lord in His Word. I have found that occasional, irregular times in the Word are less productive, sometimes even frustrating. The more time I spend in the Bible, and in relationship with the Author, the more likely I am to actually experience the Lord's light and truth. It's never too late to start building a relationship with God through His Word! One last note, though it's a big one: note where the light and truth are ultimately pointing. Straight to God, or as verse 4 says "to the place where You live." All the clarity, direction and instruction in the world, are, apart from God, rather pointless. Interesting, that while we may have been scrambling to find out what our next steps in life are, there's really only ever been one step that mattered: a step towards God!

That singular desire, to be close to God, literally answers every other question that life asks, either directly or indirectly. When I am safely snuggled up to the Lord, everything else in life, including the questions like "what's next?" are lovingly and patiently addressed. The rest of verse 4 underlines this truth: "There I will go to the altar of God, to God—the source of all my joy." I will go to God MY source, THE source.

APPLICATION ▸   Let's put into practice this simple passage right now, if you can. Linger for a moment longer with your Bible open. Slowly read verses 3 and 4 again. Open your heart and mind to the presence and awareness of the Lord. Make an inner pivot to place your attention on your loving Father, and to shift your attention away from the difficulties that want to consume you. Trust Him to bring you light and truth, right on time.

PRAYER ▸

Lord, I trust you to show me light and truth; please open Your Word to my understanding. Draw me to Yourself; speak loving direction to me. Help me to trust Your timing. Amen. So be it.

TWENTY-SIX

GOD OUR REFUGE & STRENGTH

SCRIPTURE   Read Psalm 46.

OBSERVATION   This is another one of the Psalms that I'm not quite sure where to start; there's so much good stuff here, both instantly recognizable, and some a little bit more obscure. There's a lot of yellow pencil crayon in this passage in my Bible (check the colour-coding guide at the front of this book for an explanation), a whole lot of insight into the character and nature of God. Even as a simple assist to my worship life, this is a pretty stellar chapter. Among many other attributes, it reminds me that God is:

- **my refuge** (v1): After the week I've had, this is a supremely steadying reminder!
- **my strength** (v1): I'm reminded in scripture that "when I am weak, then I am strong." (2 Corinthians 12:10) Boy, did I need to hear that these past couple of days!
- **always ready to help in times of trouble** (v1): Like I said, a great reminder: Lord, I'm waiting for Your help!
- **my joy and my protector** (v4,5): To a "Riversider" like myself, a reference to rivers like this always catches my attention (see Jeremiah 17:8 for our theme verse). Lord, bring refreshing and healing through the flow of Your life through me.
- **my fortress** (v7): Strength personified—that's our God!
- **glorious in the ways that He works** (v8,9): Now there's

a couple of libraries for the ages: the glorious, marvellous, astonishing, powerful works of our God; how much time do you have?

APPLICATION That's all well and good you might say; all of these great and awesome things about God. But what do we do about it? How can we make it part of our experience? Verse 10 provides the answer, maybe unexpectedly, maybe even a bit against our natural intuitions and inclinations. It's a beautiful and well known passage that puts all of these into practical expression; it brings things down from the mighty and majestic, the humanly unattainable, into the here and now of my next breath and heartbeat." Be still and know that I am God." (v10) What a gift this verse is: it strips away the mystery of the ages, and closes the perceived gulf between us and God and presents the simplest of tasks and methods, and grants a pathway to God that literally anyone can access. "Be still"; this will be the entry point into knowing God. Now, I didn't say it would be easy. Finding quietness in a noisy world can be challenging, no doubt about it. But it can, it MUST, be done. Before we go one second further, see if you can carve out a moment of God-focused quietness. Think about His attributes from earlier in the chapter, but mostly be quiet, be still.

PRAYER

ssshhhh…

TWENTY-SEVEN

GOD MADE KNOWN

SCRIPTURE ▸ Read Psalm 48.

OBSERVATION ▸ This psalm is a lot about the holy city, Jerusalem. As such, it may be a little difficult for a modern reader to catch the elevated importance that the "city of our God" (v1,8) held in the eyes, minds and hearts of the those who read this centuries ago. If you read carefully, you can pick up the overwhelming sense of awe and wonder that a visiting pilgrim might have experienced upon entering its walls for the very first glimpse of its sacred majesty, having spent countless hours only imagining it: "We had heard of the city's glory, but now we have seen it for ourselves…" (v8) It's that particular line that always catches my attention whenever I read this chapter: "…we have seen it for ourselves." In my Bible, that's coloured in dark green pencil crayon, which I use to highlight scriptures that relate to my own Christian experience, my personal walk of faith. Of all the colour-coding I use in my study of the Word, that's the one that always arrests my attention first, because of the recognizability—I have experienced it, and can verify that it has shown itself to be true. Now, that's not to say that every instance of dark green notations in my Bible is complete—it is called a walk of faith for a reason, remember! Sometimes I colour by faith, believing that in God's faithful and perfect timing, I will "see it for myself" (v8). This journey of faith is made infinitely easier to you and me today, because of the fact that we are followers of Jesus. (If you have not yet made the decision to become a follower, and would like to, turn to the last page of this devotional and consider becoming a believer in Jesus, using the simple prayer written there as a guide.)

Let me explain the way that Jesus makes this a reality. Back to Psalm 48, and the importance of Jerusalem as a central focus of worship. The holy city was the place where the Temple was, and that meant it was the place where God was. So, by extension, to the worshipper of God, it was the highest and best location in which to worship. That is wonderful, unless you're not in Jerusalem. Here's where Jesus comes in. Do you happen to remember a conversation that He had with a certain Samaritan woman at a well outside of the town where she lived? It's found in John 4, and the dialogue came around to a discussion of where worship is best conducted. Jesus said: "The time is coming when it will no longer matter whether you worship the Father on this mountain or in Jerusalem." With that statement, He was laying out the sweeping change in all matters of worship that He was about to deliver, through his death and resurrection: He was now going to be the object and source of true worship. No longer was it centralized by a singular, limited location. In other words, we could now "see it for ourselves"! (v8) One quick story from my past. When I attended Bible College for the first time (what happened there is another story for another day!), about the only thing I actually recall with much clarity is what one professor said regarding this thing called one's 'personal walk of faith'. I paraphrase: "The whole world can stand up and tell you that your faith in Jesus is not real; and that it's old-fashioned, out of date, weak, foolish and useless. But when you really, truly experience Him, no one can ever, ever take Him away from you." That, my friends, has been absolutely true for me, because now "...we have seen it for ourselves."

_____

APPLICATION ▶ Sometimes life and faith get complicated—this is also something else that I have experienced! I'd like to encourage you to simplify things by narrowing down your focus—to Jesus. One of the most probing questions I can ever ask a fellow believer cuts past all the noise, all the distractions, all the peripheral stuff, and moves us into the only discussion that ultimately matters: "How are you and Jesus doing?" Make that your 'application' today. Re-connect with Jesus.

_____

PRAYER ▶

Lord, help me to "see You for myself"; to really experience You again. I confess that I get distracted sometimes, and I may even ignore or neglect my friendship with You. Thank you that You never reject me or distance Yourself, that You always warmly welcome me. I rest in your loving kindness. So be it.

_____

TWENTY-EIGHT

LET'S TALK WITH GOD

SCRIPTURE ▶ Read Psalm 50.

OBSERVATION ▶ I woke up ridiculously early this morning. I slept uninterrupted until then, a deep and satisfying sleep, but when I opened my eyes, I already knew that trying to fall back to sleep would be pointless. So, I got up and settled into the best part of any day, at least for me: the still of the early morning. On days like this, I am practically giddy with anticipation, as I get myself dressed and ready for the day. I get my cup of coffee, plunk myself down in my recliner by the window, and open my Bible. It's as though I am responding to a personal invitation from the Lord to sit with Him; the quietness around me amplifies my ability to hear His voice, to sense His presence, to anticipate a sweet, inner dialogue with Him. Whether or not I discover something profound and life-changing (which is actually a fairly rare occurrence), or if the time spent was largely unremarkable, it never disappoints. I have known the truth and joy of a passage we looked at a couple of days ago: "Be still and know that I am God." (Psalm 46:10) Let me return for a moment to an assumption I make every time I engage with the Lord in this way (or any way, for that matter). I'm not ashamed to say that when I open my Bible, I fully expect to interact with the Lord –I really do. Listen, I know there are folks who would question my approach to my time spent with God; too presumptuous, too risky, too juvenile, too unrealistic, even too flaky. I've heard them all. And maybe it's solely down to the way I'm wired, and I understand how it may come across. However, I just can't shake the belief I have in the relational nature of the Lord. Like they used to say in the X Files: "I've seen too much"! This belief is rooted in the Word itself, and this chapter stokes those beliefs. Verses 1 and 3 are pretty blunt in their assessment: "The Lord, the Mighty One, is God, and He has spoken; (v1) Our God approaches, and He is not silent." (v3) The rest of the chapter is liberally sprinkled with references to communication; to speaking, to calling, to listening. Any way you choose to look at it, it appears that God willingly and happily participates in communing with His beloved children. If you'll permit me a "pastoral" teaching/experience observation my experience through the years has taught me: that most errors with regards to the topic of God speaking, happen in the extremes. Either we tend to give God too much credit for speaking, as though it is a literal non-stop running dialogue, or we lurch over to the other extreme, that God never speaks. In my experience, both viewpoints are potentially hazardous, and neither is true. For me, the safest place lies somewhere in the middle, to be held loosely in a humble, expectant heart. Keep in mind that this was written in a time in which God was much less accessible, and hearing Him speak was fraught with all kinds of challenges, sometimes downright frightening. As New Covenant believers, how thankful we can be for the indwelt presence of the Holy Spirit to assist in the ease of clearly hearing God!

APPLICATION　What's your experience been with hearing from the Lord, and communicating with Him? Do you have a preferred method of going about this? Is the concept difficult for you to envision? If you can, take a moment to ponder your experience regarding interactions with Him. Have a look back over your life and remember times in which you have sensed that God was speaking with you. Maybe putting those recollections into clear thoughts would be well expressed through a simple prayer...

PRAYER

Lord, if it's true that You speak to your children, then I'd like to experience that. I have a sense that my life would be richer and fuller with that kind of communication. Teach me how to listen and how to hear. I open my heart to communicating with You. In fact, I look forward to it. I'm glad that I do not have to fear You. Yours is the kind voice of a caring Father. Show me how to go about it, because sometimes I'm not sure. I ask this with a growing confidence in Your Word, and a growing confidence in Your love. Amen.

Listen well, dear friends...

TWENTY-NINE

RESTORE ME

SCRIPTURE ▸ Read Psalm 51.

OBSERVATION ▸ Before we go any further in this devotional, I think it would be helpful to go directly to the actual story that is being referenced in this psalm. Look up 2 Samuel 11&12, read the story, and let its gut-wrenching rawness settle around you.

Now, to today's passage (you'll note in the psalm's heading the precise correlation). It is a fairly recognizable experience in our lives when we are "found out". None of us is perfect and so there will be moments (some big, some small) in which we do things that are less than desirable, things we're not proud of, and some of these things have truly horrendous consequences. While today's scripture is most certainly a big one, let me share something of the smaller variety. The other day, my daughter heard the water running in the upstairs bathroom. As the mother of an almost three year old, her wise and trained ear instantly recognized that a follow up inquiry was in order. "Are you playing with the water?" she asked. "No, mommy" was the response. To an experienced parent (with a little less alarm to a grandparent!), the answer was almost laughable; the overwhelming evidence pointed directly to a toddler happily playing with the bathroom faucets. As cute as this story and my grandson is, it highlights something in humanity that is all too familiar. In this painful story in Psalm 51, King David, at the height of his kingly power and influence, has been exposed by the prophet Nathan. He has done something heinous and unthinkable.

Now it must be reckoned with before God, and thus begins the agonizing pathway and his permanently altered life on the way back to a restored relationship with the Lord. Note his anguish: "Wash me clean from my guilt. Purify me from my sins. For I recognize my rebellion; it haunts me day and night." (v2, 3) I bring this up not to point the finger at King David, to somehow shame his memory and excuse myself in the meantime. Regardless of the actualities of the sin in question, we are all deeply and inherently broken by sin, sinful behaviours, and their consequences. Rather, the point is the part about repentance and restoration. Understanding the dynamics and necessity of these things is critical in the life of a believer. The more we embrace this reality, the healthier we will live, as it will be in all honesty a fairly regular component of a vibrant relationship with the Lord. David captures this hope and healing by using phrases like "give me back my joy again", "create in me a clean heart", "renew a loyal spirit within me", and "restore to me the joy of your salvation". (v 8, 10,12) Even in the midst his brokenness, he remains full of confidence that the Lord will forgive and restore him; the same confidence we have today. There's a special note I want for you to recognize in the life of the king, and it really is the key to this whole story. David maintained a soft and responsive heart before God. The good news, I believe, is that it is a skill that can be developed and nurtured. That's where our Application comes in.

APPLICATION ▶ I don't think it's a stretch to say that each of us can recognize moments when the Holy Spirit taps us on the shoulder in order to point out a misstep, whether inside and largely invisible or outside and more readily obvious. The question always comes down to a very simple point: how will I respond to the Lord? Refusing to listen, act, or acknowledge the Lord's prompting is really the death knell to vibrant spirituality. Though not always easy (and I certainly don't present myself as one who always gets it right), David's example is both a simple and solid one: Acknowledge it. Repent of it. Be forgiven and restored.

PRAYER

I kind of think we just did...

THIRTY

TRUST, TRUST, TRUST

SCRIPTURE ▸   Read Psalm 52.

OBSERVATION ▸   As you may have heard or read by now, I love references to trees—especially so, when the trees mentioned are thriving! Verse 8 of this chapter is one of my favourites: "But I am like an olive tree, thriving in the house of God. I will always trust in God's unfailing love." The psalmist, David, makes this declaration as a rebuttal to a ruthless opponent who has bad intentions toward him. On the surface, it may sound to us to be a little boastful, but in context, he is simply and truthfully making a case for trusting God, and further building his faith while he's at it. Parts of what I'm about to note could quite easily fit in our "Application" segment, but I'm going to walk through it here anyway, and we'll see where we go from there.

To begin, I love the boldness of his opening statement: "I am like an olive tree…" Not being a culture that is terribly familiar with olives, nor one that sees olive groves everywhere we look, we might think it was an odd illustration. For David and his readers, they instantly got what he was saying: 'I am resilient, I am fruitful, I am life-giving, I am firmly rooted'. This is more than boasting, that is simply the true assessment and confession of any and all committed believers: you and me! Next up: "I am thriving". The key to this is where the tree is planted: in the house of God, which speaks of closeness to the Lord. It extends well past a literal place (the Temple, or in our case, the church), though that is certainly part of being well-planted. A thriving tree has put its roots down into the river of God and the flow of life that is slowly, yet supernaturally transferred from the river, through the roots, to the tree trunk, out to the branches and ultimately to the fruit itself. It is first and foremost close to God. (Riversiders would readily recognize this; Jeremiah 17:8) Which, as always, sounds wonderful; the burning question, however, remains "how?" And thankfully, David provides us with practical insight, and it shows up in the form of a couple of other expressions of faith that he had regularly practiced. It could almost be described as a simple recipe that looks like this:

- ◆ 2 parts "trust"
- ◆ 1 part "praise"
- ◆ a generous pinch of "presence".

"I will always TRUST in God's unfailing love. I will PRAISE you forever, O God, for what You have done. I will TRUST in Your good name in the PRESENCE of Your faithful people." (v 8b, 9) Can you see it? There are times in scripture when the pathway to deeper faith and robust trust is actually quite straightforward, even when presented with the complexities of life. Perhaps the only thing missing in David's recipe is the length of time it must stay in the heat of the fire! For that I would say, leave it in for a long time, a lifetime!

APPLICATION ▶ Briefly, let's look at the ingredients one last time. My dear Mom used to tell me all the time, as I was leaving her home after a visit "Son, the key to life in Jesus is: 'Trust. Trust. Trust.'" She would always say it three times. David's recipe only uses it twice, but I'm sure you get the picture. Exercise trust liberally in everything, every situation, the big, the small, in everything. Say it out loud. Say it in the face of doubt and fear. Apply it over and over, even when you don't feel like it, or when things appear to be getting worse. Trust! It's faithful application is one of the most powerful tools that God provides. There are times when it might even feel foolish or pointless, as you survey an enormous challenge in front of you, but declaring our trust in God is a bold, loud statement to the unseen world, and notably, to ourselves, that builds… you guessed it: more trust. Finally, "…in the presence of your faithful people" In case you needed help in understanding the deep theological implications here, it means: go to Church! As imperfect as Church can be at times, surrounding yourself with the "good name" of God together with other folks is divinely designed and therefore, uniquely able to deliver the supernatural!

PRAYER

Lord, let's make a delightful recipe together. Grant me the patience to let it come to fullness. Guide my life in the most honourable pursuit of trust. I choose to trust. I choose to praise. I choose Your presence. Amen. So be it.

THIRTY-ONE
YOU HAVE RESCUED ME

SCRIPTURE▶   Read Psalm 54.

OBSERVATION▶   This short psalm, including its introductory heading, is really intriguing. It's only seven verses long, but reads like a dramatic short story. The backstory is that David is running for his life from King Saul; in his growing paranoia, Saul has begun a murderous rampage against anyone who he imagines is conspiring against him, and David is at the top of the list. (2 Samuel 22,23) This psalm captures the moment when men from the town of Ziph went to Saul to betray David's hiding place. Let's pick up the story…Verse 1: "Come with great power, O God, and rescue me! Defend me with your might". A desperate prayer from a desperate man. Remember, he is hiding in a cave, literally fearing for his life. I have never experienced these exact circumstances, but I certainly recognize the sentiment! How about you? Verse 2 says "Listen to my prayer, O God. Pay attention to my plea." To paraphrase this situation: "Please God, do something! Anything!" Verses 3&5: He puts into words his situation as he prays. As I think about it, isn't that what prayer actually is? Simply a reciting of the painful, confusing stuff in our lives; but it doesn't stop there. We take that messy bundle and do our best to lift it up and leave it (without a doubt, that's the tricky part!) with God. Much like David did in…Verse 4: "But God is my helper. The Lord keeps me alive!" This short declaration of faith and belief is then underscored by a quick reference to remembering well, which is supremely helpful in times of great duress: "Do as you promised…" (5) In other words, I've seen You do it before, You've given me promises in Your Word to hold on to, so...Verse 5: "I will sacrifice a voluntary offering to you; I will praise Your name, O Lord, for it is good." I love this, because of its practicality! It is not enough for David to just talk about the situation. He is very clearly a man of action, so he throws his spiritual energy into faith-building action, in his case, a voluntary sacrifice. What that 'action' looks like for us might look different, though it will likely be very personal. However, there is one commonality we can all agree on: Praise! Verse 7: "For You have rescued me from my troubles and helped me to triumph over my enemies." This verse has a couple of noteworthy points, and they have to do with tenses:

◆ It indicates that David is remembering times in the past when God has faithfully delivered him. This builds his faith in this present dire situation.
◆ It also demonstrates that his faith is being put into action right now. He is speaking as though these outcomes have already happened!
◆ Envision this: as he huddles in the cave, hardly daring to breathe, as enemy troops are circling around, he states: "You HAVE rescued me..."Now, that's faith!

APPLICATION ▶ Take a moment, especially if you're going through a difficult season, and re-visit this story as reflected in this short psalm. Pattern your responses after what David did, and the model he provided. Pray, be honest about the situation, praise (that might feel like the greatest sacrifice of all), remember God's promises and His faithfulness in times past, keep moving forward in faith, no matter how incremental...

PRAYER

Lord, I may not be literally hiding for my life in a cave right now, but it kind of feels familiar anyway. I'm looking to You. I don't know how You are going to deliver me, but because I know You, I believe by faith that You can and You will! Help me in the moments that I waver and feel weak. I believe You, Lord. Help me in my unbelief. Amen.

Bless you, dear friends...

THIRTY-TWO
"HEART" PSALM

SCRIPTURE ▶   Read Psalm 57.

OBSERVATION ▶   I think I've said this couple of times before, but this psalm is truly one of my favourites! It is one of the things that has consistently spoken to me; or perhaps more accurately, to my heart. Let me briefly explain what I mean by that. It's not terribly uncommon in our experience to hear people describe the somewhat mystical, inner, unseen function of the "heart". Of course, we realize that we're not talking about the literal, physical vital organ called a heart (though these things must be confusing for folks who are new to English—if that's you, bless you on your journey, dear friend). What is being described is an inner quality; an expression of an individual and their character. It is a glimpse into the real person, past the outward and easily seen physical attributes. Yet, as invisible and difficult to pin down exactly what it is, it is at the same time quite readily apparent. We could say things like: "He's got a good heart", or "She's got a soft heart", or perhaps even something negative, like "a black heart." This passage contains several mentions of the heart, and when I see those, they immediately capture my attention. First off, I love the childlike dependence that I see in verse 1: "…I look to You for protection. I will hide beneath the shadow of Your wings." I suppose some might not like that feeling, but for me, it's comforting. I'm okay with feeling helpless, with needing to find a safe place to snuggle up. God's "wings" will do just fine for me! What assurance comes from verse 2, where David writes that he emphatically believes that

God will "fulfil His purpose for me". At the risk of belabouring the point, remember he is recalling a pretty horrific time in his life; and yet, a heart submitted to God allows a quiet confidence and trust to arise, that God is committed to partnering with me for the long haul. Verse 3 reminds us of the character and nature of our Father; one who sends us "unfailing love and faithfulness." Let that massage itself into your heart today! Slowly now: He will NEVER fail us! The heart shows up front and centre in verse 7 and 8: "My heart is confident in You, O God; My heart is confident. No wonder I can sing Your praises! Wake up, my heart!"

Now, I realize that this inner condition of the "heart" can sometimes be directly connected to the way that God put each person together. Without question, some folks find this a more natural, intuitive thing; some do not find it so easy, and may genuinely struggle with issues associated with the "heart". This is most often reflected in the language of things like "hearing" God and "listening" to the voice of the Lord. (In case you hadn't guessed, I am one of those who is predominantly guided by the "heart", and it's pretty plain to see that David was as well.) Nonetheless, I believe that this inner attitude and posture towards the Lord is something that can be developed and embraced, no matter how you are assembled! David says as much when he uses words and expressions like:

- **"I look to You"** (v1); That's an inner leaning, a purposeful action one takes.
- **"I cry out"** (v2); Communicating with God, on whatever level.
- **"Be exalted, O God"** (v5); The faith-building action of praise.
- **"I sing Your praises!"** (v7); Again, doing something tangible to express trust in God.

- **"I will thank You"** (v9); Another deliberate action, and a powerful, attitude-shifting one at that.
- **"...among the people...among the nations..."** (v9); the power of being influenced by other godly people.

Read: go to Church to work on your "heart" condition—you'll be surrounded by others trying to do exactly the same thing! In truth, anyone can do these things, regardless of how they are put together, and that's encouraging for all of us.

APPLICATION ▶ Actually, I think we just did. Or, if you feel the need, go through it again, thoughtfully and prayerfully.

PRAYER

Same again—I think we just did. Bless you, dear friends, as you offer the most precious part of who you are to our loving Father; your "heart".

THIRTY-THREE

AN INHERITANCE

SCRIPTURE ▶ Read Psalm 61.

OBSERVATION ▶ My brother and I recently received the news that probate was completed with regards to our parents' will. The whole process has had me pondering first, of course, the legacy of my parents, and secondly, the similarities in such things with our Heavenly Father. With that in mind, verse 5 of this chapter really popped out: "For You have heard my vows, O God. You have given me an inheritance reserved for those who fear Your name."

Just like we experienced a few years back with my wife's wonderful parents, we are about to receive an inheritance; the fruit of my mom and dad's life and labour. This is very humbling, and I struggle with finding adequate words to capture the broad considerations of this faithful, thoughtful and generous act. Mostly, the key is just to hold out one's hands, and…well, receive. The truth is (and I suppose this is the humbling part) I did nothing to deserve this. The act of grace and giving is solely dependent on them; their quiet dedication to their family and to the Lord resulted in something tangible to be passed on to their sons, and beyond. More than the tangibles, however, are the intangibles that they passed on. These things may not have a dollar value but are increasingly rare these days; I would contend that they are actually priceless. A partial list would include things like kindness, generosity, decency and respect for others. We watched through the years as our parents modelled these to the best of their abilities, the traits that believers would recognize as the "fruit of the Spirit." (Galatians 5:22,23) Thanks, Mom and Dad!

Now, let's shift over to the similarities with God, who, like a caring and attentive parent, has set something aside: an inheritance. This is actually fairly common language in the Bible, especially so for societies around that time in history— caring for your family was one of the highest values imaginable! (If you'd like to view a few more examples from the perspective of spiritual inheritance, flip over to Psalm 16:6, Ephesians 1:14, Colossians 3:24, Hebrews 9:15) As is the case with my folks, we do nothing to deserve this generous gift from God. There is another consideration here, and it's a big one, that sets apart our heavenly inheritance from an earthly one: it lasts forever! Unlike an earthly inheritance, which is finite—it only goes so far, it only lasts for a certain amount of time. When all is said and done, it will run out; as I said, it's finite. As Hebrews 9 states "…so that all who are called can receive the eternal inheritance God has promised them." And if there's one thing we can take to the bank regarding God and His character, He keeps His promises!

APPLICATION   Back in the day, accessing your eternal inheritance was straightforward, though not necessarily easy.

The first and last part of verse 5 bear this out; note the requirements: "You have heard my vows..." and, "...an inheritance reserved for those who fear Your name." So, the inheritance was conditional: if you do these things (make and keep vows, and fear God's name), then you will qualify. Such was the way of the Old Covenant; here are the rules and conditions—now get to the business of working with all your might to keep your part of the agreement! As I so often say, thank God for the New Covenant! More akin to my parents and their will in this way, is the promise that God gives. The promised inheritance has nothing to do with my behaviours, or my "earning". It is simply promised and given out of love. What do you think our "Application" should look like today? Maybe a simple "thank You, Jesus", followed by a humble re-commitment to walk alongside Him is enough...

PRAYER

Thank You, Lord, for the New Covenant that You have given us through Your shed blood. Thank You, Jesus, for the promise of unfailing friendship in this life and eternity with You in the next life. Grant me the grace and strength to walk closely with You. Amen.

Keep walking, dear friends...

THIRTY-FOUR

QUIETLY I WAIT

SCRIPTURE ▶ Read Psalm 62.

OBSERVATION ▶ This psalm has a lot of really good stuff in it, much of it giving insight into the character and nature of God, which by extension, always builds our faith. It's worth a read just for that alone. In this case, however, I'd like to ponder another component of it, one that provides some very practical direction into making our relationship with God more readily experienced. Two verses basically deliver the same message in this regard: verse 1 and verse 5. "I wait quietly before God, for my victory comes from Him." (1), and "Let all that I am wait quietly before God, for my hope is in Him." (5) Those simple instructions, to "wait quietly" are really at the heart of the matter. As with so many instances in scripture, achieving this state is both simple and challenging. Let's unpack it a little further.

Off the top, be encouraged: I don't think there's hardly a person in the world that isn't capable of quietly waiting. Then why does it seem like such a huge stretch? Two things come to mind: First, to do so requires intentionality and focus. The world around us happily plays its part in loudly demanding our attention, in keeping our minds and souls constantly bombarded with messages that are quite opposed to both the state of quietness and the prospect of waiting. Yet, to those who take a moment, to those who are spiritually intrigued by the whispered hope of this possibility, (indeed its promise of deepened intimacy with the Lord) the opportunities are all around us. Maybe the most encouraging part of all, because scripture declares it and models as much, it is achievable by you and I today. I suspect that how one goes about carving out time and space to embrace quietly waiting is probably the easiest part of the whole equation! The key is found in some sort of purposeful action, no matter how small it might be.

They are really two parts of the same reality in the life of a follower of Jesus, so let's not overcomplicate it: take time to quiet yourself, and then posture yourself inwardly to wait; which is really another way to say: "Lord, I trust You and I trust Your timing." A quick word to the wise: this "waiting" is most certainly not a one-time declaration, and knowing that may be the key. Do not be ashamed or embarrassed if you find yourself handing over your anxious thoughts to the Lord a hundred times a day as you wait. It's simply a part of the process of learning the skill of waiting for the Lord.

_____

_____

_____

_____

_____

_____

APPLICATION I said there were two things that came to mind, so here's the second one, which is also the most critical consideration: the 'Who' that I'm waiting before! Never forget that we're talking about the Lord here. Sometimes lost in the translation of trying to practically figure things out in the happy and welcoming context of relationship (thank you New

Covenant!), is the remembrance that we're still talking about Almighty God! God happens, by the way, to invite us to wait quietly before Him, as He does in our lives what only He can do. The psalmist said as much: He's the only One who can bring victory (v1) and He's the ultimate source of all my hope (v5). So what precisely is our application, then? I would recommend finding some quiet time at some point today, and practice waiting for the Lord. This much I know: He will show up!

PRAYER

Lord, teach me to be quiet, and please teach me to wait. I'm so grateful that You are the embodiment of patience, because we're going to need it! Teach us to trust; You are our only hope of victory. Amen.

THIRTY-FIVE
I SEEK YOU GOD

SCRIPTURE ▶ Read Psalm 63.

OBSERVATION ▶ I'm getting ready to head out the door in a few minutes to meet an old friend for breakfast. The opportunity to get together showed up rather unexpectedly and I'm genuinely excited to connect and catch up! The only time we could meet was very early in the morning; he had much family business to attend to while he was briefly in town. And so, I set my alarm early (as is typical of me, I woke up well before the alarm sounded) and eagerly slid out of bed. With a growing sense of anticipation, I did my usual morning stuff, all the while keeping one eye on the clock—I didn't want to miss one moment of our allotted time together. When I read Psalm 63 today, it reminded me of something that pertains to my own spiritual life; something similar to the sense of anticipation I felt regarding meeting up with an old and dear friend. While the previous psalm (62) was all about "waiting" for the Lord, this passage bumps things up a notch: this psalm introduces another aspect of relationship with God—"seeking". Truthfully, this component of my walk of faith has been a little more hit-and-miss than some others. I'm not completely sure why that is. Maybe it's that there are more distractions in our modern lives than there were when David lived, or perhaps he just possessed a depth of hunger for God that I simply do not. Either way, he had within him a longing to know God that was pretty extraordinary. "O God, You are my God; I earnestly search for You. My soul thirsts for You; My whole body longs for You in this parched and weary land where there is no water." (v1) It helps with the visual imagery to remember that David wrote this while in the dusty, dry wilderness of Judah—he equated an intense physical thirst he was experiencing to the inner spiritual longing to be close to the Lord.

As I thought about these things this morning, it dawned on me. While I might not fully understand the concept of seeking or searching for God, this much I know for certain: the moments in my life that I have had that sensation of eagerly desiring to pursue God, to really, truly want to know Him better, to "long" for Him; those times have produced the most impacting, lasting, memorable moments of growth in me. Conversely, I thought about how there have been somewhat large swaths of time in which that keen desire to seek him has been absent or at least muted. Much of my time and effort is spent somewhat passively, lounging about complacently; content to just "be", content for Him to come to me. Now, He regularly does, and for that I'm very thankful. But, I'm left with a distant longing for something more…

APPLICATION ▶ I'm usually fairly certain of what to write in this section of our little devotional time; less so this morning. There is a perceptible stirring, a deepening desire within me to move toward a new era of approaching my relationship with the Lord. I suppose I'm looking to find a balance between the "waiting" and the "seeking". Maybe verse 6 holds a key: "I lie awake thinking of You, meditating on You through the night." Verse 8 expresses that attitude of craving and deeply, almost desperately, needing God: "I cling to You; Your strong right hand holds me securely." One last thing. When I was a young adult, in the dawning of the age of contemporary Christian music, there was a band called the 2nd Chapter of Acts, who recorded a song called "Psalm 63". That song has remained embedded in my heart and mind for all these years; to the point that it was actually present and fundamentally foundational to the formation of the church I now pastor, Riverside. (there was even a day in which I used this song as my alarm wake-up...) If you're interested, you might want to have a listen; I think that's going to be my personal application today. I'm going to go for a walk and listen to it again; I'm also going to ask the Lord to teach me to search and seek again.

PRAYER

See above. Bless you, dear seekers of God...

THIRTY-SIX
ABUNDANT RIVER OF GOD

SCRIPTURE ▶ Read Psalm 65.

OBSERVATION ▶ This is a psalm of abundance. Virtually every line tells of the ways which God lavishly pours out His blessings, whether in nature, or into the lives of those following Him. Any way you slice it, God has lots and lots of everything! Let's just wander through the chapter, and be encouraged as we note the many ways He shows this.

Off the top, there's a couple of references to "answered prayer" (v 2,5), and the interactions between those who pray (us), and the One who answers (God). Those interactions are easily recognizable: we praise (v1), we serve (v1), we come to Him (v2), we sin, He forgives (v3), we rejoice (v4), we pray, He responds (v5), we hope (v5), we wander (v5). Sound familiar? Quietly inserted in the last part of verse 2 is a stand-alone line, which is pretty significant and also pretty comprehensive: "All of us must come to You." That's a great reminder for us as believers, and a telling statement for every person in the world, pointing towards an inevitable eventuality: when all is said and done, God will have the final say.

For me, as a follower of Jesus, I take that and simply direct my attention and energy to making that as much of a reality now as I can. I try to practice the discipline and enjoy of reality of walking moment to moment with Jesus, as best as I can. As often as I can, I come to Him, just like verse 2 says. Verse 6 and onward speak of the Lord's greatness and generosity regarding His creation, both plants and animals. For someone wired like me, this is one of the most sure-fire ways of seeing the abundance of God at work: observing nature, in all its bigness, and in all its smallness. I recently officiated a wedding on the platform of the Sea to Sky gondola, near Squamish, B.C. The stunning magnificence of the setting made it quite difficult for the assembled guests to not be distracted from the presumed focal point of the day—the bride! Such was the indescribable majesty of the mountain and ocean views. As I read this morning, it was easy to catch the glory of God, as the psalmist describes mountains (v6), oceans (v7), sunrise and sunset (v8), rivers (v9), grasslands and meadows, hills and valleys (v12, 13). Wherever you find yourself, take some time to seek God through His abundance, whether it's in person, or from a picture, or even from a memory—He is displayed through His abundant creation!

One last note about our Father's abundance, and again, it's kind of slipped in, as a treat for those who are watching. It's found in verse 9, and references a river; but not just any river. A very unique and special river: The river of God and I think it's appropriate that any further discussion of that river fall under the heading of...

APPLICATION ▶ The idea of a "river of God" is not unusual, nor is the idea uncommon in the Bible. It is called this by name and as a concept, it is referenced quite frequently. I believe that it is meant to illustrate an aspect of the same abundance that we have been exploring in this devotional, this time with an emphasis on the way a river brings life, health and vitality to those who access its waters. That's how it is with the "river of God": in other words, there is a flow of life that comes straight from God. Unlike a physical, earthly river, because of its Source, this river never dries up and provides generously, produces rich and fruitful harvests, and makes everything around it fertile and healthy (v9). It even turns hard ground and wilderness areas into lush and abundant pastures (v11,12). Such is the way life with the Lord works. Simply being close to Him brings life and health. Take some time today to purposefully get closer to that river, however that looks for you. As I wrote this today, my experience was that as I pondered these things regarding God and His abundance, I was able to do just that: get a little closer to the "river of God".

PRAYER

Lord, help me today to move closer to You, to drink deeply of the satisfying river that is You; a river that will never dry up, no matter what is going on in the world. I'm thankful for that. Amen.

I might even go and sit by a river at some point today.

THIRTY-SEVEN

REMEMBERING WELL

SCRIPTURE ▶   Read Psalm 66.

OBSERVATION ▶   I had the joy of re-connecting with old friends the other day. I use the word "joy" intentionally, as it was present with such great abundance; lots of laughter, lots of filling in the blanks of stories long forgotten, lots of fond and affectionate reminiscing. The number one phrase on our lips seemed to be: "Hey, do you remember when…?" Without a doubt, there is a certain power in remembering well; even painful memories, when handled respectfully and submitted to God have the capacity to clarify and heal.

In matters of faith, remembering well goes even further than that. It is no less than the key to building, maintaining, and expanding our faith moving forward. Our psalm for today demonstrates all of these things. The first few verses set the stage (1-3): giving God joyful praise, founded upon recalling what God has done in the past. "Say to God, 'How awesome are your deeds!'" This is literally the fuel that propels faith! Simply put, if you want to live and function with a greater, more robust attitude of faith, take time to remember well what God has done in your life! (I think you can probably guess what the "Application" segment is going to look like today!) Verses 5 through 12 tell two different stories from Israel's past; remember, this psalm is being composed around about a thousand years after the two stories took place—talk about faithfully re-telling the faith stories of that people's history! Both stories come from around the time of Moses, and the great Exodus from captivity in Egypt. The first is the miraculous crossing of the Red Sea (v 5-7; Exodus 14); the second is the broader story of their ultimate rescue and deliverance from the chains of slavery (v 8-12; basically, the whole book of Exodus). Verse 13 then starts with the word "now", which is really the spring-board into the action step that follows the recounting of stories that highlight God's faithfulness. In other words, what do we do next? In the case of the psalmist, the next steps seemed rather straightforward: putting into practice the work that is necessary to make his faith vibrant; to willingly and actively participate in the activities that surround his personal walk of faith. For him, it was things like bringing offerings and fulfilling vows (v 13), giving the best of his resources, even if it meant sacrificing something costly (v 15), sharing his faith and testimony with others (v 16), and ensuring that confession and repentance were included (v 18). These were all part of his commitment to God, and following through with those commitments inevitably resulted in, you guessed it: deeper, richer faith.

APPLICATION   I draw great encouragement from verse 19, and I believe it's a both a great reminder and a great model. "But God did listen! He paid attention to my prayer." Never forget:

our relationship with God is a partnership. Sometimes we get a little confused about who exactly does what in this partnership, but the truth remains: we're in this together, and God does respond to our contributions. Why don't you list a few things that God has faithfully done in your life? Lift those up to Him in thankful remembrance and watch Him build your faith! I'm not sure that I can think of anything simpler than that.

_____

_____

_____

_____

_____

_____

PRAYER

Lord, help us to remember well, because sometimes we're a little forgetful. While we work on our end of the partnership (and we know that sometimes it doesn't feel like much), we thank You in advance for what You're doing to build up our faith. Amen, so be it.

Remember well, dear friends...

_____

_____

_____

_____

_____

_____

THIRTY-EIGHT
CONTRASTS & COMFORTS

SCRIPTURE ▶ Read Psalm 68.

OBSERVATION ▶ This psalm is one of contrasts; it progressively moves between things that are difficult and even bad, and then straight to things that are pleasant and good, and back again. Let's look at a couple of these contrasts, and then settle on one significant understanding that is helpful to all of us today.

Let's start by remembering the context and time in history that this is being written. It was a time when warfare was common and most everyone had seen or experienced bloodshed. Life seemed much cheaper back then; there were no government programs to take care of the disadvantaged, no social agencies to advocate for the destitute. In reality, there were only two sources of assistance: family and God.

Those who were fortunate enough to have a supportive family nearby were among the blessed. Many did not have this support, which left dependence on God. That of course, is still the hinge point of life, regardless of what period of history we live. That commonality knits together believers across the ages, and brings a tangible, fresh sense of hope and encouragement. Keeping that in mind will help us catch the heart of God in the midst of it all. It will also prove invaluable when we find ourselves in desperate situations.

To our psalm, and the first contrast: the wicked and the godly (v 1-5). As always, God invites everyone into His Presence to enjoy life in Him. He leaves the choice (it is a regular choice, don't forget) to each one of us. Make sure you choose well! Another contrast is found in verses 7-10: wilderness versus abundance. Again, a life of faith in God is offered to all, and once chosen, must still be lived and experienced through countless decisions throughout our Christian lives. Unfortunately, many believers make the choice to accept God's offer, but thereafter, continue to dwell in the wilderness. If that sounds familiar, choose again today to reignite your relationship with the Lord!

There's a broad description of contrasts throughout the rest of the chapter, and those have to do with the imagery of war and armed conflict; it uses language like "enemies", "rebellion", "captives" and "armies". Its counterpoint is found in a verse like this: "Praise the Lord; praise God our Saviour! For each day He carries us in His arms. Our God is a God who saves! The Sovereign Lord rescues us from death." (v19,20) And that's the place I'd like to settle on today. The wonderful imagery of our Lord carrying His beloved children, and carrying us from war to peace, from fear to faith. Any parent (or in my happy case, grandparent!) can easily envision that moment of tender compassion and caring, when a little one is scooped up and held close, and given comfort and security.

APPLICATION ▶   So, let's allow that to sink in and wash over us today. How do you go to the Lord for comfort when you need it? Are there things you do, or places you go that assist in the process? Are there certain songs or specific Bible verses? I know that I have utilized all of these and many more besides. I suppose that's my takeaway for today: re-envisioning my connection with Jesus. Here is a final thought on "contrasts"; whether I'm going through a rough patch right now, or I find myself on top of the world, I desire that my approach to life would be the same: carried in the arms of my faithful God!

_____

_____

_____

_____

_____

_____

_____

PRAYER ▶

Lord, help me to never lose that precious sense of childlikeness in my life. Even now, help me to come to You, with an expectation of being safely and lovingly carried to wherever we need to go today. I trust You, Lord. Amen.

_____

_____

_____

_____

_____

THIRTY-NINE

DESPERATE TIMES

SCRIPTURE ▶ Read Psalm 69.

OBSERVATION ▶ There are a couple of things that immediately catch my attention upon reading this psalm; I'd like to bring them to you, so we can consider them together. The first is the sheer, raw desperation that is front and centre in David's writing. It actually kind of takes your breath away when you first read it—there's no soft entry point here, no easing in by gradual degrees. It veritably screams out in the very first verse: "Save me, O God, for the floodwaters are up to my neck. Deeper and deeper I sink into the mire. I can't find a foothold. I am in deep water, and the floods overwhelm me". That is one of the most visceral, gut-wrenching descriptions of the turmoil life can sometimes bring our way. It doesn't really even matter how the situation arose; it is unimportant whether we contributed to it, or we were unwittingly subjected to it. All we know is that it feels a lot like we're drowning; we actually have real concerns that we might not survive. Reading a passage like this actually has strange a way of bringing along with it a sense of comfort; it's really quite a remarkable thing, sometimes tangible and intangible at exactly the same time. Just hearing someone else say it, especially when it was articulated in such vivid and recognizable words can be a comfort in itself. It's also very helpful that David doesn't languish for very long in the agony of his situation. He is always moving towards God, in some way, shape or form, and that's super important to note. Consistently moving toward God is another key to faith; it may be small steps (it usually is, by the way), but it is movement, nonetheless. In fact, notice that his first words, just before he launches into the description of his turmoil are directed to God: "Save me, O God…" (I glanced ahead to the next chapter, and he does exactly the same thing again: "Please, God, rescue me!" (Psalm 70:1) That's consistency!

The second note in this chapter that stood out to me has to do with the nature of prayer, as David understood it, and it takes place in verse 13: "But I keep praying to You, Lord, hoping this time You will show me favour." I can see where some might view his prayer as a little feeble. After all, wouldn't you think that one of the great characters of faith in the entire Bible would be able to muster a little more faith and power? I'm not troubled by that; in fact, I'm strengthened and encouraged by his honesty. It certainly resembles times that I have prayed in desperate situations, oftentimes because I simply had no other options. To utilize David's imagery, it was either sink or swim by faith! Ultimately, I suppose that difficult moments like this are actually the proving grounds of faith. No one is suggesting that they are fun; they're not. They may, however, be more necessary and productive than we can hope to understand in the moment.

APPLICATION ▶ Let's practice the art and discipline of predictably turning toward God. No matter what you're presently experiencing (or enduring!), take a moment to inwardly turn toward the Lord. Even if all you can squeak out is a faint "Save me, rescue me, O God", just like David did, do it. You may be surprised by the strength and hope that follows! Be assured that God hears, and that He cares.

_____

_____

_____

_____

_____

_____

PRAYER ▶

I guess something like:

"Save me, rescue me, O Lord," will more than suffice. Let our "amen" be: "Answer my prayers, O Lord, for Your unfailing love is wonderful. Take care of me, for Your mercy is so plentiful." (v 16)

Bless you, dear friends...

_____

_____

_____

_____

FORTY

SAVE ME

SCRIPTURE Read Psalm 71.

OBSERVATION From time to time, I find myself the victim of a little bit of cynicism. Part of that is because I tend to find humour in most things, sometimes inappropriately so (I'll spare you any examples!), and my sense of humour is capable of some darker shades. On a more spiritual note, another consideration is that the walk of faith is regularly challenged by life's circumstances.

Prayers that go unanswered, or at least appear to be so, coupled with lots of sad circumstances all around us, can create a kind of spiritual apathy that makes it easy to shrug our shoulders and sigh "whatever". This is simply a reality in the walk of faith of every Christian, and it has a way of ebbing and flowing with the passing of time. Ultimately, of course, God is utterly faithful and completely trustworthy; it's our human understandings that often cloud the true picture and gnaw away at our foundations of faith. There's a simple statement in this psalm that I find incredibly encouraging, a statement that immediately restores proper perspective regarding my faith; every time I come across it, it leaps from the page and significantly adjusts my thinking, even though it's actually less than half of a verse. Here it is: "Give the order to save me…" (v3) There's a lot in those six words, if you stop to consider them. First, let's remember who the author is addressing, and as we've alluded to before, the context of the writing of those words. It's a part of a longer prayer, so we know that David is in the act of praying; we've been given a front row seat to witness his personal struggle, and centuries later, we still receive the benefits of his honesty and the modelling of his faith. He weaves his requests between reminding God (and himself) of God's own qualities and then projecting those characteristics forward onto the problems at hand. It's really a remarkable demonstration of faith in action! He consistently follows this same method for the rest of the chapter—watch for it. Remind and remember, appeal and petition.

Secondly, there is a settled-ness, a finality, in that one short line that speaks volumes regarding his view on God, and it's that certainty that affects me whenever I see it. Let me paraphrase: "Father God, because of who You are, because of Your limitless power and unfailing love towards me, I bring my problem/concern/crisis to You. I believe that nothing is too difficult or too complicated for You, and You alone have the true and proper perspective on things. Therefore, I believe that You are able to "Give the order" to set things right in my life. Literally one word from You is enough to radically change everything! Because You alone have the knowledge and authority over everything on earth, You alone are capable of making changes, big or small, outward or inward. Whether You do that instantly or whether it takes a longer time than I'd like, the foundation of my faith declares that You can. And so, I trust in You. Faith compels me to state along with David, 'Give the order to save me'!" Or something along those lines. Can you see yourself mustering up the faith to mirror his hope-filled request?

_____

_____

_____

_____

APPLICATION This seems to me to be fairly straightforward: take whatever it is that you are struggling with and lift it up before the Lord. It doesn't have to be fancy or eloquent; David often makes that clear enough! For me, it takes me back to my childhood, and those innocent, impressionable years when I truly believed that my Dad could do anything. It's pretty much the same thing.

PRAYER

I suppose you could simply repeat back my paraphrased prayer of a moment ago. You could construct your own, or you could simply read back to God the ancient petition of someone very close to Him, but still very human. "Give the order to save me, for You are my rock and my fortress." Bless you on this leg of your journey…

FORTY-ONE
SANCTUARY & SHELTER

SCRIPTURE Read Psalm 73.

OBSERVATION Though this psalm is written by an author other than David, it is remarkably consistent in its imagery, and in its vivid account of navigating life's difficulties. Ultimately, the author Asaph comes to the identical conclusions as David: the only safe place to reside in life is with God! A few chapters earlier, in Psalm 69 primarily, David used the imagery of being swept away by a raging flood. His descriptions were incredibly real; we could almost feel his overwhelming sense of panic, figuratively gasping for air while clawing for a safe grip, helplessly fearing that he was about to drown. This passage further describes that sense of desperation but does so after the immediate danger has passed. "But as for me, I almost lost my footing. My feet were slipping, and I was almost gone." (v2) When I read this, it restores within me a sense of hope and optimism. It gives me the benefit of observing this truth in the lives of those who love and follow God, whether that's today or centuries ago: God faithfully and carefully guides our lives to a "glorious destiny". (v 23,24) In the next section (v3-20) Asaph basically wrestles with the injustices that he sees in the world around him; the often-unresolvable issues of fairness and cruelty, of those who have plenty, and those who have next to nothing. His musings did not necessarily lead him to complete and tidy answers. Instead, he interrupts his train of thought with one magnificent statement, a key spiritual truth that we still do well to heed: "Then I went into Your sanctuary, O God, and I finally understood…" (v17) Our best defence, the surest place to be, especially in the face of tumult and uncertainty is in the presence of God; that's really describing the things we do to establish intimacy with the Lord. These things might look different to you than they do to me, but I would suggest that there are most likely some strong threads of similar, recognizable things that would be practiced by believers the world over. (One of those things is what we're doing right now: seeking the Lord's presence through His Word) Verse 23 strikes another chord of deep assurance: "Yet I still belong to You; You hold my right hand. You guide me with Your counsel, Leading me to a glorious destiny." I recognize this pattern of human experience, and I'm sure you do too. After we list our complaints and ailments to the Lord (bringing "complaints" before the Lord is fairly common human practice, just so you know. Flip back a few pages and read the first verse of Psalm 64), we arrive at a critical faith-juncture: do I stay mired in my complaints and unhappiness, or do I direct my energies (or whatever may be left of them!) to moving towards God, my Source and strength? That's really another relatively simple key to faith: choosing to orient ourselves with God's Presence, in spite of the difficulties that may be raging around us.

APPLICATION　　This is a perfect moment to pause and put this into practice. I'm assuming that if you're reading this right now, you've probably got your Bible open and your thoughts are largely directed towards the Lord – that's half the battle! Maybe the best application of all is to simply not hurry away back to the crush of life and busyness. Pause. Take a deep breath. Review this passage. And pray…something like this…

_____

_____

_____

_____

_____

_____

_____

PRAYER

Lord, thanks for providing hope through the lives and stories of those who have gone before us. Encourage us today through the Word, and in Your presence; remind us of Your power and faithfulness to deliver us safely and securely. Help us when we get distracted by fear and anxiety. Teach us to trust. Amen. So be it

Find your rest in His presence, dear friends…

_____

_____

_____

_____

_____

FORTY-TWO

SANCTUARY & SHELTER (PART 2)

SCRIPTURE ➤ Read Psalm 73.

OBSERVATION ➤ Man, does this passage cover the expanse of a believer's experience! Hope, frustration, the seeming inequities of life, bordering on futility...then refocused hope and restoration. I especially love verse 17a: "Then I went to your sanctuary, O God..." That's both the literal sanctuary of the House of the Lord and the quiet, personal place of refuge I find alone with Him. Also, verse 26 "My health may fail, and my spirit may grow weak, but God remains the strength of my heart; He is mine forever."

APPLICATION ▶ What comfort comes with that understanding and acknowledgement: God is mine forever. No matter what happens today, my Heavenly Father will be there! Say it to yourself; say it out loud: "God is mine forever!"

_____

_____

_____

_____

_____

_____

_____

_____

PRAYER ▶

Father in Heaven, help me to recognize your loving Presence today. Please remind me when I forget. Write those words on my heart: You are mine forever!

_____

_____

_____

_____

_____

_____

_____

FORTY-THREE

DARK TIMES

SCRIPTURE Read Psalm 74.

OBSERVATION The bulk of this Psalm is pretty dark and discouraging. It's obviously written in a desperate time, when hope and fond memories are in short supply. In the middle of the bleakness of their present situation, the author pulls out a pillar of true and deep faith: reminding God of His promises, especially those that reflect 'covenant' (v 20). When all seems lost, this is what Bible heroes of old did: they reminded God of what He had promised! (That's not to suggest that God forgot-it is solely for the benefit of the person doing the reminding!)

APPLICATION There's a healthy chunk of "remembering well" in this passage (verses 12-17). Sometimes this feels like one of the only things we are capable of in really tough times —remembering God's faithful power in times past. While it may seem almost insignificant, it's actually huge in the life of a growing follower of Jesus. It's a key to worshipping well and to navigating difficult times. This is a discipline, for sure; most often, it's not my initial inner reflex. As we mature in the Lord, however, we find ourselves getting to that place of health and hope more readily and in a shorter time span. This would be a good moment to pause for a second and remember God's faithfulness with thanks.

PRAYER

Father, I remember your goodness and faithfulness. You have never failed me or deserted me, and you never will. Help me to remember well in moments of weakness or distraction. Thank you that I am safely in Your care!

FORTY-FOUR

GOD'S CHARACTER

SCRIPTURE ▶ Read Psalm 75.

OBSERVATION ▶ In my Bible, any reference to God, His character, His nature, or His actions is pencil-crayoned in yellow. (Check out the colour-coding guide that I use at the start of this book.) This particular passage has lots of yellow, but also some yellow that is really helpful in instructing me. For example:

- ◆ vs 1 "...you are near..."
- ◆ vs 1 "...your wonderful deeds..."
- ◆ vs 2 "...at the time I have planned..."
- ◆ vs 2 "...I will bring justice..."
- ◆ vs 7 "...God alone who judges..."
- ◆ vs 7 "...He decides who rise and fall..."

There are other examples, but there's some pretty amazing attributes of God there!

APPLICATION ▶ As I look around at the state of the world, this relatively short passage brings immense comfort. If even one of those observations about God is true (verse 1 reminds me that God is near; as simple as that concept/truth is, is there a more powerful understanding in the life of a believer?), that can completely change my perspective; most importantly, it can allow me rest and trust in His character, no matter what craziness might be happening around me. Try to apply the Word in a way that comforts and strengthens you. That's what it's meant for!

PRAYER ▶

Father, I thank you for your Word, that shines truth into dark places. Strengthen and encourage us; teach us to trust; help us to wisely apply your promises to our life situation and help me to share my growing trust and confidence in You to those around me.

FORTY-FIVE

FOR THE WEARY

SCRIPTURE ▶ Read Psalm 77.

OBSERVATION ▶ I am regularly surprised by the raw honesty of the Psalms. They so vividly encompass the breadth of the human experience, don't they? I was reminded of that as I read this morning. Now I am sitting here, pondering a particularly painful chapter in my life as I write this, remembering the crushing hopelessness I felt. I share this with you in the hope that you might be encouraged on your journey, especially if you are experiencing some challenges to your faith.

As I look at the passage as a whole, I see it as a glimpse into the Psalm writer's diary. The first part describes the utter sense of despair that we have all felt at some point in our lives. As hard as we have tried to follow the Lord, to obey, to listen, to pray, even to sacrifice, it appears that it has been pointless; "my soul is not comforted." (v2) Then, a few moments of back and forth, as though the writer is trying to will himself back into alignment. Note how he uses 'remembrance'—recalling God's faithful promises of the past. A brief slip into despair again: This is my fate; the Most High has turned His Hand against me." (v10) And then, finally, the scales tip, the penny drops, and a conscious decision is engaged: "But THEN I RECALL all you have done, O Lord; I REMEMBER your wonderful deeds. " (v11)

APPLICATION ▶   It's okay to despair. If we're honest, every single one of us has been in that awful place. The key to surviving and re-discovering hope-filled perspective is to resist the urge to languish in that place for an extended period of time. Then, as feeble as it seems and as hopeless as things still might appear, we stumble forward in faith, just like the writers of old. It doesn't feel like much, but I have seen God honour that expression of faith in my own life, and many others lives as well (it even includes a verse that Ingrid ministered to me at a particularly low point (v19)). The rest of the chapter assists in re-calibrating our faith in the light of God's powerful faithfulness.

PRAYER ▶

Thank you, Lord, for your tender patience with me. Even in times when I have felt like giving up (or actually did momentarily give up!), You never gave up on me. Help me to remember your faithfulness to me and my family, to me and my faith-family. Grant comfort and strength to those who are faint or weary.

Bless you today, dear friends...

FORTY-SIX
STILL MY SHEPHERD

SCRIPTURE Read Psalm 79.

OBSERVATION As you may be aware, the book of Psalms in our present-day Bible was composed by several authors; hence, it reflects different and unique personalities, styles and life situations in its pages. The chapters we have just encountered are written by Asaph; styles and themes are notably different than those written by the more familiar, and more pastoral, King David. Suffice to say, Asaph is having a bad day! Or a few of them! Lots of anger, lots of frustration, lots of hoping for revenge—all expressed in the context of somewhat rambling history lessons. But there is a point; amidst the sharp language he uses, both chapters 78 & 79 wrap up with a comforting return to the solid ground of the Lord as 'shepherd'.

APPLICATION There is something to be said for honest dialogue with the Lord—it really should be the point of prayer, right? From my perspective, it seems that our friend Asaph is a little wound up, but who am I to judge? However, he is honest, and that's something I strive to be in my walk with Jesus. Sometimes I think I hold back a little in my prayers, as though I think maybe God can't bear the really hard stuff, or as though prayer is mainly a confession of my ineptitude and I'm really embarrassed at the notion of not appearing capable as a mature adult—in other words, quit whining and just try harder! I guess the application is this: we will all have 'Asaph' days at some point. Sometimes they are brief, sometimes they seem to span years. Either way, be encouraged to bring your best and your worst to the Great Shepherd—it's in the character and nature of the Shepherd that shelter, hope, and comfort is found.

PRAYER

Read Psalm 23 as your prayer, slowly and thoughtfully. Envision yourself as a sheep, and the Lord as your shepherd...literally.

FORTY-SEVEN
ROOTS

SCRIPTURE Read Psalm 80.

OBSERVATION Anytime I see the imagery of trees in the Bible, especially references to roots and rivers, it immediately catches my attention. Riversiders will be aware of this, because the founding verse of our church is Jeremiah 17:8 (look it up, when you have a moment). Naturally, bumping into verses 8 and 9 caused my usual thoughtful pause; "....we took root and filled the land." What follows predictably is a question to ponder: "What goes into a healthy root system, for either a group of people, or an individual?"

APPLICATION Even for an amateur gardener, there's a basic understanding of the roots of a plant, or in the case of this passage specifically, a vine. The roots are the critical conduit system that transports water and nutrients to the visible parts of a plant, most notably the leaves and the flowers or fruit. Without a healthy root system, there is simply no possibility of fruitfulness. Here's my one main take-away from this picture today: the roots are largely unseen and unnoticed. They seem almost unconnected to the vibrant beauty and fragrance of a flower, or to the delightful sweetness of a piece of fruit. How true this is of my own spiritual health.

My inner life, unseen by most, is where the key to my outer, visible life lies. As I write this, I sit by myself on the porch of our holiday log cabin in Parksville, probably a full hour before anyone else in our beloved family stirs. That simple act of faithful and anticipatory seeking, repeated countless times, has allowed God access to my heart and spirit, giving Him some room to work, shape and mould my 'roots'. The encouraging thing is that it's never too late to start that inner partnership. As we say at Riverside every time we open our Bibles together: "...I choose to open my heart to receive a word from God that changes my life forever."

PRAYER

Repeat what you just read...the part about choosing to open our hearts to receive...and pray accordingly...

FORTY-EIGHT
SET YOUR MIND

SCRIPTURE ▶   Read Psalm 84.

OBSERVATION ▶   Okay, I've got to be honest with you: I'm kind of done with our friend Asaph and his songs and musings of war and retribution towards his enemies! I promise you, I did read Psalms 81-83, but I'm going to pause here this morning for a psalm of encouragement from the 'descendants of Korah.' (Psalm 84)

First off, what a dramatic shift in atmosphere in this Psalm! Almost instantly upon reading, I can feel a renewed sense of joy and hope. This really is an instance in which we can experience the 'aliveness' of the Word (Hebrews 4:12). Something really caught my attention in this passage, in the latter part of verse 5; those who have "set their minds…" What a simple, yet powerful truth: setting your mind, especially on walking closely with Jesus, is something that anyone can do. It's a purposeful action. It's not reserved only for the 'super spiritual', for the professional, for the highly educated, or for those who have a title that we would associate with Church. In my experience, it's not a one-time occurrence, or something done in an emotional moment in a church service (though it could most assuredly happen there too). It's a simple, repetitive, submitted act of the heart, will and mind. When engaged regularly, it becomes a very natural way of approaching life's journey and a real way to experience the rest that God promises His children! (Hebrews 4:1,3,6,7,9)

It's a profoundly wonderful thing to have a "set" mind!

APPLICATION If you think about it, it's what you're doing as you read your Bible along with me right now! Especially wonderful is the 'setting of your mind' first thing in the morning, as I am privileged to be doing as I write this. It seems to set the day's compass on the right bearing. It signals to me and to the Lord that my intention is to actively include Him in my day, wherever it may lead.

PRAYER

Father, help me today, in the all-too-common crush of a busy and demanding world, to 'set my mind' on You. Teach me; I desperately need to learn the art and skill of this beautiful reality. Grant me the opportunity and the wisdom to discover this joyous, rest-producing practice. Amen.

FORTY-NINE

FULL OF GRACE AND TRUTH

SCRIPTURE ▶ Read Psalm 85.

OBSERVATION ▶ This is another psalm that reminds us of the stark differences between the Old and New Covenants. That's made clear by the seeming sense of fickleness that God displays toward His people (more or less described in verses 1-7). Be assured, God is not fickle; the reality and operation of the Old Covenant simply had a 'back and forth' about it, that made our position in relation to God constantly shifting. It was based on law and rule-keeping. But that's not actually what I wanted to share with you today! (As I often say to our beloved Riverside people: "That was free!")

Okay, here's the part of the passage that jumped out at me: "Unfailing love and truth have met together. Righteousness and peace have kissed!" (v 10) My spirit leapt inside me as I read that because it's talking about Jesus! (orange pencil crayon here!) Here we are hundreds and hundreds of years before Jesus physically walks the earth, and the Psalmist is perfectly describing Him! My mind immediately went to John 1, where Jesus is magnificently described this way: "So the Word (Jesus) became human and made His home among us. He was full of unfailing love and faithfulness." Can you see the similarity? Elsewhere, the NIV translation renders this as "full of grace and truth". 2 Peter 1:1 calls Jesus "just and fair." I've got to admit, I can hardly sit still to write this! The author is describing our friend, our hope, our peace, our everything—Jesus!

_____

_____

_____

_____

APPLICATION▶   I recently was asked to speak at a worship event. I'm not yet sure what I'll speak about exactly, but when I do, there will be a generous helping of the person of Jesus. He is the reason we worship and He is the reason we can know God. Even though we're technically reading in the Psalms right now, perhaps a refresher might be in order, as to the pre-eminence and majesty of Jesus. Why don't you flip over to John 1:1-18, and let that inspire and shape your worship? Maybe that's all we need to know: the person of Jesus. That experienced knowledge that comes via relationship, and the changed heart that inevitably accompanies it, is the heart of true worship. It's all that really matters. He's all that really matters!

_____

_____

_____

_____

PRAYER▶

> _Jesus, may we see you more clearly today. Whether it's in the pages of songs written thousands of years ago, or in intimate moments today, may we know you, and your "unfailing love and truth"!_

_____

_____

_____

_____

FIFTY

PRAY

SCRIPTURE ▶ Read Psalm 86.

OBSERVATION ▶ I've been thinking a lot about prayer lately; partly because of a short series on prayer that we're going to do shortly and partly because I'm simply being stirred to engage with the Lord more fully and more broadly than I have before. Whatever the reason, this psalm (which is a return to David's authorship) jumps right into the deep end of the prayer pool! As we prayed together recently, at All Church Prayer (something we do every month at Riverside), we hung out pretty extensively on the first component of prayer found in verse 1: "...I need your help." This is so refreshingly typical of David's direct approach to God, and something that builds a quiet, determined confidence in the act of Prayer.

Help! We simply lifted up to the Lord areas of our lives in which we, or others we know, need God's help. I think sometimes in our supposed sophistication, we intellectually or emotionally dance around the basic premise of prayer:

I can't do this (whatever that is) by myself; I don't have the capacity or the resources to address this; I'm not capable of carrying this load. Which is, of course, humbling and aligning in the same breath. That confession aligns me with my Heavenly Father and releases the proper flow between 'need' and 'provision', between my humanness and God's "God-ness". Later on, in verse 6, David reiterates: "... hear my urgent cry. I will call to you whenever I'm in trouble." Pretty stark reminder and example, isn't it? One of the most powerful, accomplished and notable people in the entire Bible, unashamedly and intentionally spells out his utter need and childlike dependence on God.

APPLICATION In a word, pray! How often I have been guilty of the "prayer as a last resort" approach, only to remember at the close of the day, "maybe I should have prayed about that!" As David Benner wrote: "Prayer is more than you could ever imagine, because God is so much beyond what you can conceive. We are surrounded by gods that are too small to be up to the task of holding our deepest personal longings, never mind the world's most urgent problems." Indeed.

PRAYER

As the disciples said all those years ago: "Lord, teach us to pray." That still holds true today. Lord, teach us to pray.

FIFTY-ONE

CONFESSION

SCRIPTURE Read Psalm 89.

OBSERVATION First off, this is a comparatively long chapter of 52 verses. In it, the author journeys through a couple of distinct passages which are often marked by the notation of an 'interlude', between them. It wouldn't be a mistake to view the entire passage as a musical movement—that was most likely its original intent. It begins with a remembrance of the Lord's faithful promises via covenant with King David (v1-4), morphs into a section that extols the magnificence of our Heavenly Father (v5-14: try to read that without rejoicing in praise!), pauses briefly to describe the worship experience of a follower of God (v15-18), jumps into lengthy treatise on the God's covenant with King David (v19-37), then painfully recounts its human failure (v38-51), and mercifully brings it to a close with a brief, one verse reminder of Who is in charge (v52)! Whew! What a ride! This psalm is like so many others—it allows a glimpse into the common human experience (albeit most of us are not earthly royalty), complete with its broad range of emotions, including successes and failures, joys and heartaches.

APPLICATION ▶   Rather than focus on a single passage or verse, let's allow the broadness of the entire psalm to wash over us, almost in the form of a 'confession'. Let's imagine ourselves in His Presence, the palms of our hands up in a posture of release and receptivity, with a heart that is open and honest; recognizing the complexities of our lives and yet embracing the totality of God's grace and love that completely covers us.

PRAYER

A prayer could sound something like this:

"Father, I come before you with the knowledge that my life can be messy and full of moving parts, often comprised of conflicting realities. Some of these are powerful certainties, while some are frightening uncertainties. I lift up to you the entire package: the good, the bad, and the ugly. In faith and trust, I thank you for your unchanging care in my life. I thank you that no matter what happens, I am secure in Your Love. I declare and confess (say this out loud!) that YOU ARE ENOUGH. Amen."

FIFTY-TWO

THE "PROPORTIONS"
OF GOD

SCRIPTURE ▶ Read Psalm 90.

OBSERVATION ▶ Everybody loves to get a great 'deal' when they go shopping and we especially love to tell others about it! There's something about our understanding and appreciation of value—the profitable exchange between me and a vendor, of my money for their product that leaves us both quite satisfied. Psalm 90 contains a reference to a similar type of exchange, except in this case, it's between God and me. It gives us some insight into the heart of our generous Father and the way He views it.

The actual verse is Psalm 90:15, and it contains a fascinating word: "proportion". "Give us gladness in proportion to our former misery," the psalmist prays. This is what came to me, and I wrote it in the margin at the bottom of the page in my Bible: "God's proportion is never our proportion. His contribution is always 'exceedingly, abundantly, above all we could ever ask or think…" Ephesians 3:20 (KJV). In human context, I would generally be happy for a "one to one" exchange; an exchange that I would determine to be fair and equitable; reasonable; acceptable; or a good 'deal' even… But not our Heavenly Father—It's never "one for one" with Him! That would be far too 'human' for Him, far too limited, far too contained. What a beautiful picture of the heart of God! Unlike the exchange of goods and services between people, where we are overjoyed at the occasional appearance of a great 'deal', God generously, lavishly, repeatedly, almost recklessly, pours out His idea of proportionality towards us. Think about it: my sin, exchanged for His forgiveness; my pain, for His joy; my past, for His promised future; my poverty, for His riches; my fears, for His hope….and on and on it goes. I say again: His proportion is NEVER my proportion, praise God!

APPLICATION ▶   May we each get a further glimpse into the incredible, astonishing, immeasurable depths of God's grace to each of us today; and may that glimpse draw us deeper into His loving embrace, strengthen our faith and trust and dispel our fears.

PRAYER ▶

"Give us gladness in proportion to our former misery! Replace the evil years with good." Thank you, Father, that you are immeasurably generous! Amen.

FIFTY-THREE

PRACTICAL STUFF

SCRIPTURE Read Psalm 92.

OBSERVATION

Boy, does this psalm resonate with me, on numerous levels! Let me briefly pull a few personal notes out for you.

- ◆ **v1:** what a simple, great reminder: it's a good thing to give praise and thanks to God. 'Nuff said. Do it, Terry!
- ◆ **v2:** I love the references to the times of the day; morning and evening. I happen to be spending time with the Lord early on Friday morning, and by evening, I will certainly have much more to thank Him for!
- ◆ **v4:** this actually instructs me on how to approach and experience verses 1&2—by consciously and regularly remembering what He has done, and saying it!
- ◆ **vs 12&13**: any passage that talks about trees flourishing instantly grabs my attention; see Jeremiah 17:8 to review and compare Riverside's theme verse.
- ◆ **vs 14&15**: as I age, this promise (highlighted in light green, my 'promise' colour, in my Bible), brings a hope-filled perspective moving forward into the future.

APPLICATION ▶   Kind of what we just did! Take time to thoughtfully and prayerfully ponder the various thoughts in the chapter. I find that carving out a space in which I am not in a hurry is a huge key. For me, busyness is the enemy of my spiritual growth and health, while intentionality is my friend.

PRAYER

Lord, it is so good to spend time with you in the Word. Thank you for always receiving me when I seek you; thanks for patiently waiting for me, even in stretches when my busyness momentarily distracts me. Finally, thanks for meeting me so tenderly this morning.

FIFTY-FOUR
HOW LONG?

SCRIPTURE Read Psalm 94.

OBSERVATION Verses 3 and 4 contain perhaps the most often uttered question in the life of believer: how long? Every one of us, as we learn to walk in partnership with God, has asked this same question, usually as it relates to a particularly difficult passage of life. Whether it's an illness, a financial squeeze, the painful journey of a loved one or unfair treatment at work, whatever the situation, the question is: how long will this last, Lord? I think what makes it particularly difficult is the knowledge that it's God who is our partner. He is Almighty, All powerful and all knowing. The conundrum is this: if You are all that and more, Lord, why don't You do something? Fortunately, the biblical record and personal experience teaches us that God is indeed listening and active. In fact, over time, we will often come to understand that some of His most outstanding and life-changing work is done in precisely these agonizing life passages.

APPLICATION▶   Here's where it gets really practical, and therefore very encouraging! In short succession, the psalmist lists a bunch of truths about our Father that deliver much needed, hope-filled perspective in tough times. Such as:

- **v10**: "He knows everything…"
- **v11**: "He knows people's thoughts…"
- **v12**: Priceless gifts of discipline and teaching are taking place
- **v14** "He will not reject…He will not abandon…"
- **v18,19:** Maybe all we need to know in the "How long?" moments in our lives: "I cried out, "I am slipping!" but your unfailing love, O Lord supported me. When doubts filled my mind, your comfort gave me renewed hope and cheer."

PRAYER

Let's simply re-read verses 18 and 19 and present them as a prayer. So be it.

FIFTY-FIVE

HEART POSTURE

SCRIPTURE ▸   Read Psalm 95.

OBSERVATION ▸   This psalm presents two quite different perspectives on relationship with God, which as written can be a bit confusing. Thankfully, we are the recipients of the New Covenant, which helps our understanding and reduces (actually erases, more accurately!) the angst we might feel when we approach the Father. First, verses 1-7(a) are an encouragement to come to God in worship, most likely based on some past experiences when the psalmist was present in moments of passionate, rapturous praise and worship. It sort of parallels my own experiences, for as I age, I have come to treasure more and more the beauty of worshipping together with the Body. I always purposefully position myself in the front row of our congregation, mostly to 'feel' the worship of my faith family washing over me, as though in waves.

Now, the contrast; verses 7(b)-11 come across as a rather stern lecture and warning, which, of course, is warranted based on the recorded events following the great exodus from Egypt and the ensuing journey towards the Promised Land. Lest we view it as only a history lesson and an inner "tsk, tsk…" directed towards those ancient pilgrims, I find the words have almost always struck a chord in my own heart, and the directive lands in a very personal spot in my own life and heart. "If only you would listen to His voice today" the passage pleads. (v7(b))

APPLICATION ▶ That, then, is my application for today. To carve out time and space to humbly walk with a heart posture of actively and intentionally listening well, and on the heels of that, to obediently respond. How you do that is entirely up to you. I suspect that your life looks quite different from mine. However, it's the urgency in those words that catches my attention and moves my heart. May it gently, yet strongly, do the same for you.

PRAYER

Craft a prayer that reflects the 'Application' above, the intentional and purposeful posturing of a soft heart and listening ear. The prayer might start with "Lord, help me to do this…" I know mine frequently does. Bless you as you listen well today…

FIFTY-SIX
SCRIPTURE AS PRAYER

SCRIPTURE ▶   Read Psalm 96 & 97.

OBSERVATION ▶   As I was reading here this morning, I found myself breezing right past the chapter and verse notations and reading as though it was one uninterrupted passage. That's a little bit strange for me; I tend to look for small details, waiting for even a single word to capture the attention of my heart, and then pausing and pondering, often for hours or sometimes even days. The majesty of this passage seemed to present itself as a sweeping anthem of praise. I could imagine all of heaven belting it out in a collective declaration of God's worthiness and that I was being personally invited to join in! In my Bible, as you may know by now, I colour-code fairly substantially. (Again, you can glance at the little colour-coding guide at the front of this book, if you like) The predominant colours of these two psalms gives evidence of what I was just sharing: yellow tells of the character and nature of God, and red highlights the response/expectation of a follower of God (me!). These particular chapters ebb and flow between yellow and red: His greatness, my worshipful response...oh, and by the way, there's way more yellow than red! What a beautiful, natural way to begin my day-being reminded of our incredible, wonderful Heavenly Father, and then converting that reminder into joyous, expectant praise!

APPLICATION ▶   Try following that template. Hum it, sing it. At the very least, speak it out loud. Relax in the Holy Spirit and allow the power and truth of the Word invite you into this most healthy life posture…these two Psalms are a great snapshot of the perspectives that make up the pathway to an ever-deepening walk with the Lord. Honestly, if you were to spend the rest of your devotional life only in Psalm 96 and 97, you wouldn't go far wrong!

PRAYER

How often scripture is best viewed as Prayer. Quiet yourself and offer this passage (v8) as your heartfelt prayer to your awesome Father.

FIFTY-SEVEN

ACKNOWLEDGING THE LORD

SCRIPTURE ▶   Read Psalm 100.

OBSERVATION ▶   Not to belabour the methodology for my personal Bible Study, but this particular passage contains a lot of 'red' passages. This tells me at a glance that it contains practical instruction for living life as a Christian, as a follower of Jesus, a child of God, and as someone who desires to deepen their walk of faith and love with their Heavenly Father. So, in the order in which these 'instructions' appear, let's get started. (I briefly hesitate to use the word 'instructions', lest this appear so trite as a checklist, or some tasks to be performed—the directions provided in this psalm are life-giving helps; the gaining of wisdom; provision for comfort and security; health and nurture to my soul and spirit; all while being practical, logical and plainly written down! Anyway, I think you get the point...)

- **v1**: Shout with joy—a great reminder of the act of praise, and a director of my focus: "to the Lord". Amazing how praise, in all circumstances, does that!
- **v2**: Worship the Lord with gladness. A deep reverence, reserved for God alone, that very naturally produces gladness. Both 'praise' and 'worship' often have a sacrificial component to them, but are all the more powerful and faith-producing when offered in tough situations.
- **v2**: Come before Him: the act of intentional pursuit of God.

It speaks of humble desire and something I've noticed through the years—God seems to really embrace this!

◆ **v3**: Acknowledge: Again, intentionality. Think it, say it: "You alone are my God". Use whatever language you choose, but something powerful is released when we simply acknowledge Him.

◆ **v4**: Enter His gates with thanksgiving, go into His courts with praise. Let's not lose the truth and reality of this passage simply because it's so recognizable. Purposefully set time aside at some point today to honour Him!

◆ **v4**: Give thanks: Enough said.

APPLICATION I suppose we could just re-read the Observation, and do what the Word instructs, right?

PRAYER

I suppose we could just re-read the Application and consider it offered as prayer, right?

FIFTY-EIGHT

LET'S LINGER LONGER

SCRIPTURE Read Psalm 100.

OBSERVATION If I may, I'd like to linger in Psalm 100 a little longer. Remember, spending time in the Word is best experienced as an unhurried exercise, rather than a sequence of numbered chapters to be crossed off a list in a furious hurry to get to the next one. Anyway, as I revisited Psalm 100 this morning, something caught my eye again, as this particular imagery tends to do. It's found in the last part of verse 3: "We are His people, the sheep of His pasture." Anytime that the Bible references 'sheep', I'm all ears. That's because the Lord hard-wired me to be a pastor; a shepherd. (Please understand—I'm not bragging or pulling rank—it's just a fact, plain and simple. Not fancy, not impressive, it just is.) So, when I read and pondered that line over the last couple of days, my mind immediately cross-referenced one of the clearest descriptions that the Great Shepherd gives regarding sheep and shepherds: John 10. That passage is worthy of much more attention than I'm going to give it here, but it's main emphasis, as I see it, are the qualities of listening and following. (I've noted it in the margin of my Bible as: "Note: Voices".) Jesus provides tremendous, clear insight into the 'sheeply' skills of listening and following, which, when you come to think of it, is not really a skill at all. It's simply instinct. Sheep have a phenomenal ability to identify voices, especially the one that matters most to them, their own shepherd.

Which, I believe, is the point: developing over time, such an intuitive spiritual ear to the Lord that it requires virtually no effort whatsoever! In other words, simply listening and following.

APPLICATION This should be pretty obvious! Let's put into practice some listening skills; the good news is that if you're following along with these simple devotions, you're already engaged in doing exactly what you need to do. Really, the only skill required is a bit of time management and the rest becomes second nature to a sheep! (One hint: quietness really helps....)

PRAYER

Lord, thank you that You make these concepts easy to understand: sheep contentedly grazing while following a trustworthy shepherd. Help me to develop a listening ear, and a trusting heart

FIFTY-NINE

INTENTIONALITY

SCRIPTURE ▶ Read Psalm 101.

OBSERVATION ▶ What strikes me about this psalm is the intentionality of the author, David. Intentionality has been a really significant word in my vocabulary lately; both for me as an individual, and then by extension, as a pastor. For probably 3 or 4 months now, virtually every time I pray, or think about the body of Christ, or crack open the pages of my Bible, that concept is front and centre. To a degree, I think it has something to do with the prodding wisdom of my life coach, George, as well as the Holy Spirit's relentless work in my life, but whatever the source, I'm grateful. For far too long (I've encountered this in many others lives, too), I've simply 'hoped' that things would change; dreamed of the day when my attitudes would better manifest health; imagined what the lordship of Jesus might look like in my life's journey…. This passage reminds me of the power of purpose! Phrases like:

- ◆ "I will sing…" (v1)
- ◆ "I will praise…" (v1)
- ◆ "I will be careful to live…(v2)
- ◆ "I will lead a life of integrity in my own home…" (v2)
- ◆ "I will search…" (v6)

These all speak of intentionality, and intentionality naturally produces results. Knowing the flow of the Psalms, we know that these intentions are not simply things to do when life is going great. Most likely (read ahead to Psalm 102), these disciplines were developed in difficult times, when it took significant faith-commitment to keep moving forward. Nor were the results necessarily immediate! However, learning to live in the power of purpose is just that-a powerful thing! It's the antidote for the rampant entitlement we see around us in society. It's the power to break the bonds of victimhood that so many suffer from. Especially when that intentionality is applied to Godly and Biblical endeavours. There's a reason that we've heard, for lo, these many years, the repeated, implored instructions: read your Bible, pray, give, serve…fill in the blank here…right?

APPLICATION ▶ Pretty straightforward, I think. We could simply take one or two of the "I wills" listed earlier and put them into practice. For example, regardless of what you are going through today, "I will sing of your love and justice, Lord." Put on a worship song right now and sing. Be blessed as you experience the power of intentionality!

PRAYER ▶

Lord, grant us the grace, wisdom and the perseverance to be intentional. Thank you for your promises to partner with us in these efforts. Give strength and hope to the weary. Amen.

SIXTY

CONNECTIONS

SCRIPTURE ▶ Read Psalm 102.

OBSERVATION ▶ The longer I live as a follower of Jesus, the more connections I see; links between the Lord and my life. I used to rarely experience, or just vaguely recognize these connections; it was cause for much inner excitement and wonder when I ascertained that it had occurred. Now, I certainly never want to lose that sense of inner excitement, but I'm coming to understand that He is far more deeply and intimately connected to me than I ever dreamed possible! Those amazing moments of "wow, I just had that thought/just read that verse/ just sang that song/just prayed that prayer/just heard that at church" are so frequent that it's hard to keep up! Have you had a similar experience?

Take for example, our devotional passage for today—Psalm 102. I'm sitting in my favourite chair on Monday morning, "recovering" after preaching yesterday, when I read "Lord, hear my prayer!" (v1)

(The topic of what I've been preaching on recently? Prayer!) I guess some would chalk this up to coincidence, but as a follower of Jesus, I tend to put little stock in that—it's far too random, far too haphazard for a God who has "precious thoughts about me." (Psalm 139:17)

I choose to operate in the growing belief and experience of

God's desire to literally partner with me/us in every aspect of life, from the profound to the mundane. So, when I get up on Monday, preparing to start my week walking closely with Him, eagerly looking for evidence of that partnership, and I read that verse…wow! My faith soars, my tiredness dissipates a little more quickly and I am strengthened by the distinct sense that the Lord is right here with me, faithfully leading the way, even to the point of encouraging a little preacher in Port Coquitlam.

APPLICATION   This particular month-long series is going to be heavy on practical application. No sense yammering on for five weeks and not actually doing anything with it, right?

So, the application is pretty straightforward, and I believe it starts with an assumption: that God is with me, in me, more accurately, and loves to partner with me. Therefore, I say: "Lord, hear my prayer…"

Speak to Him what is on your heart and mind.

PRAYER

I think we just prayed…

SIXTY-ONE

LINE BY LINE, TRUTH BY TRUTH

SCRIPTURE Read Psalm 103.

OBSERVATION Now, that's the way to start a day! Psalm 103 reads like the credits that roll at the end of a blockbuster movie!

Greatness after greatness, mercy after mercy, attribute after attribute, Psalm 103 flows from one incredible insight and remembrance to the next, an ongoing highlight reel of our amazing God.

- ◆ He forgives all my sins…(v3)
- ◆ He heals…(v3)
- ◆ He redeems me…(v4)
- ◆ He crowns me…(v4)
- ◆ He fills my life with good things…(v5)
- ◆ He gives righteousness…(v6) And on…and on…

My heart literally swelled with joy and appreciation as I read that this morning. Here's why a list like this is so valuable, indeed so necessary; verse 2 gives a quick glimpse into a sad part of our human nature: forgetfulness. "May I never forget the good things He does for me." It's shocking sometimes to realize how chronically forgetful I can be. And when that happens, complaining, bitterness, comparing and self-pity are usually not far behind!

APPLICATION ▶ Let's slowly recite the psalm again; line by line, truth by truth. I love that the entire passage is 'book-ended' by this little exercise: "Let all that I am praise the Lord." (vs 1&22) Starting with a deep breath of purposeful praise is a great way to align my heart to settle under the powerful truths listed here, and thereby position myself directly under the cleansing flow of the Word of God. Roll credits!

PRAYER

Father, thank you for Who you are; thank you that I am your friend. May the truths that I read in this psalm wash over me, again and again, in order to produce faith, hope and joy! Amen!

SIXTY-TWO
GETTING TO GOD

SCRIPTURE ▶   Read Psalm 104 & 105.

OBSERVATION ▶   I love the different vehicles (chariots, I suppose!) that the psalmist drives to get to the same location, in Psalm 104 and 105. Psalm 104 arrives at the destination of praise to the Lord via thoughts about the glory of God's creation; Psalm 105 utilizes a sweeping history lesson to achieve the same goal, inciting praise and honour to the Almighty. It only makes sense that the vastness of our Heavenly Father can't be contained in a single method or manner—He's simply too multi-faceted, too magnificent, too all-encompassing. So too, our approaches to Him could and should be.

For example, at Riverside this month, we're journeying through a series on Prayer. One of the things we're discovering is the freedom that we experience when we shed narrow, restrictive approaches to prayer; that it must necessarily look, sound and feel a certain way, at a certain time, perhaps at a certain volume, take a certain amount of time, or carry a certain tone, using certain words. We concluded last Sunday's time together by sharing a "Wow" moment; something that God has done that we've witnessed and are sharing with another person in order to give glory to God and to build another's faith. Sounds an awful lot like prayer, doesn't it? What a joy to more deeply discover that there are many beautiful ways to approach our Father in prayer. As the Psalms teach us, there are also many creative, artistic, illustrative, heartfelt ways to enjoy friendship with God through His Word!

APPLICATION ⟩ Take a few moments to slow down to read again and visualize the two Psalms mentioned today: 104 & 105. Imagine the glory of creation; envision the powerful history of Israel. Utilize the spectacular imagery and descriptions to produce praise and honour to God!

PRAYER ⟩

To quote:

"Search for the Lord and for His strength; continually seek Him. Remember the wonders He has performed, His miracles, and the rulings He has given" Psalm 105: 4,5

SIXTY-THREE

ON A JOURNEY

SCRIPTURE Read Psalm 107.

OBSERVATION As I sat in church this past Sunday, I had a couple of moments when I got a little misty, thinking about the miraculous composition of the Body of Christ. Psalm 107 outlines some of the stories of our life journeys, and then thunders a repetitive theme: God redeems people, no matter where their lives have taken them! It brought to mind the passage in Colossians 3:7 "… you used to do these things when your life was still part of this world." Let me be clear; I count myself at the front of the line. Pastoring would not be very kind or productive if the approach was always directed to "you people out there"!

As this Psalm unfolded, I noted the individual journeys that are mentioned:

- The exiles (v3): who hasn't felt like a forced evacuee at some point, a stranger in a strange land?
- The wanderers (v4,5): "…lost and homeless, hungry and thirsty…" Been there, felt that.
- The prisoner (v10): whether literal or figurative, I identify with the imprisoned. Every one of us has experienced bondage and slavery, in one way or another, certainly most profoundly through our sin.
- The foolish (v17): Where to start?
- The traveller, the adventurer (v23).

On the surface, seemingly a little more noble than some of the others, but how often have I busied myself with admirable activity, when inwardly I was avoiding the Lord? Can you say "Jonah"? Can you say "Terry"? Can you see yourself anywhere in that list? The point is not to make us cower in shame—that would be completely in opposition to the good news of the Gospel! The point is found throughout the psalm, especially in the latter parts: to bring hearts of praise and gratitude to the Lord for His redemption and deliverance, and to utilize those great stories of mercy and grace to share hope with others around us! (v1,2,8,9,13,15, 20,21, 22,29,30,31,32,33,36, 38,41,42,43....I think you get the point!)

APPLICATION▶ Read Psalm 107 again, thoughtfully, prayerfully and thankfully. You might want to jot down dates and events in your Bible's margins to help you remember.

PRAYER▶

See Application—press "repeat".

SIXTY-FOUR
PROVE IT, LORD

SCRIPTURE ▶ Read Psalm 109.

OBSERVATION ▶ This psalm is a little tough to read. A beleaguered leader, subjected to cruel and bitter opposition from his enemies. It sounds similar to the vicious, personal attacks that we often hear about in modern media.

Our focus today is not that, however. What caught my eye is an intriguing line in verse 21: "But deal well with me, O Sovereign Lord, for the sake of your own reputation." The verse holds several noteworthy truths, but it's the last part that really jumped out, and brought to mind another passage, in the form of a cross-reference: Numbers 14:17. I bumped into that particular verse a few years back, and it has been a guide to my prayer life ever since. It reads: "Please, Lord, prove that your power is as great as you have claimed." I have mentioned to my flock before that it is both the safest prayer ever, and in the same breath the most dangerous prayer ever! In that particular case, Moses was the one praying. He humbly approaches God ("Please, Lord…"), but then throws down the faith gauntlet: "…prove that your power IS AS GREAT AS YOU HAVE CLAIMED." Yikes! I still flinch a little bit when I read that. Who knew that Moses had a cheeky side! But really, isn't that the essence of a prayer offered in faith? I have discovered, over the course of my life, that simply presenting the promises of God back to Him, is the most powerful, honest, and well, "safe" prayer there is. To paraphrase, "Well, Lord, didn't You say in

Your Word...?" Back to Psalm 109: "...for the sake of Your reputation..."

APPLICATION I mentioned in a message recently that I used to view Prayer and Bible Reading as two quite distinct disciplines. Here again, we see that they are really one and the same. Prayer, by offering the Word back to the Lord. Bible reading, offered as Prayer... Think about that for a moment, and give it a try!

PRAYER

"Please, Lord, prove that your power is as great as You have claimed." May the Lord bless your heartfelt pursuit of Him today!

SIXTY-FIVE
JESUS IN THE PSALMS

SCRIPTURE ▶ Read Psalm 110.

OBSERVATION ▶ I love Old Testament passages that reference Jesus! I love them for the faith-building component that they bring. Think of it, centuries before Jesus actually walked the earth, prophetically inspired authors were comprehensively describing His glory! For me, more significantly, and more personally, is the rising up of praise and thanksgiving I feel in my heart as I am "re-introduced" to Him! It's a little bit hard to describe—just when I think my heart is utterly full of love and affection for Him, I bump into a psalm like this, and a little more space is carved out for even more! Especially wonderful are passages like this that are further verified in the New Testament, kind of a "before and after" picture, if you like.

Verse 1 is quoted in Hebrews 1:13. Verse 4 is quoted in Hebrews 7:21. (Take a moment to sneak a look!)

It reminds me of what John wrote at the conclusion of the book of John: "Jesus also did many other things. If they were all written down, I suppose the whole world could not contain the books that would be written." (John 21:25)

APPLICATION Set your mind and heart on Jesus...take a deep breath...and re-read Psalm 110, verses 1, 2, 3, 4, & 7. Ponder the majesty of Jesus. Offer Him your praise. Give yourself to Him again. Allow Him to expand your heart with love. Worship the Victorious One (7)!

PRAYER

Jesus, my friend, my Saviour, my Lord. Thank you for loving me. Teach me to love you more fully. Grow room in my heart for more of You, and may that added space be expressed by deeper trust and faith. Amen.

SIXTY-SIX

START YOUR DAY

SCRIPTURE ▶ Read Psalm 111.

OBSERVATION ▶ If nothing else, this is another in a long list of psalms that is simply a great and encouraging read to begin a day! I happen to be pondering it early on a Sunday morning, before I head off to church, so verse 1 immediately pops out: "…as I meet with His godly people." The next couple of verses follow a recognizable pattern in the Psalms; listing some of the amazing attributes of God, then using those observations to move us to ponder (v2) and remember (v4), which elicits praise and builds our faith! Great design, don't you think? More glorious God characteristics come next (v5-7), then a practical encouragement for living life in partnership with Him: "…to be obeyed faithfully and with integrity." (v8) My Bible is then marked with a bright splash of orange pencil crayon (the colour I use to denote any reference, Old or New Testament, to the person of Jesus) in verse 9. "He has paid a FULL RANSOM for His people. He has guaranteed HIS COVENANT with them forever." This is a reference to the New Covenant that is coming in the future for the author and his hearers when this psalm was written, and is now the current and everlasting reality of everyone today who has agreed to the terms of the covenant; in other words, those who have accepted Jesus' offer of salvation by faith, through His death and resurrection! The ransom is paid in full: the "sin-hostages" are free! Slipped in at the end of verse 8 is perhaps the greatest understatement of all time: "What a holy, awe-inspiring name He has!" Ya think?

_____

_____

_____

_____

_____

APPLICATION Nothing fancy needed here; no extra resources, no seminary training necessary, no minimum period of time needed to understand this. Just a humble, grateful heart, and listening ears. Mix in a little faith, a growing trust, and…enjoy the blessings of a Father who loves you so much that He paid a ransom (Jesus) to set you free!

_____

_____

_____

_____

PRAYER

Lord, thanks for the truth and encouragement of Your Word. Help me to more fully embrace the truths we read today, and to get another glimpse into the glory of the New Covenant! Teach me to walk in freedom! So be it!

_____

_____

_____

_____

SIXTY-SEVEN

FRUITFULNESS

SCRIPTURE Read Psalm 112.

OBSERVATION This is a very interesting and encouraging psalm; it is largely comprised of a discussion and pondering of 'fruitfulness.' In nature, a plant's fruitfulness is dependant on several factors: soil quality, proper care of the plant itself, the removal of weeds and pests, and the availability of proper amounts of sun and water. There are notable parallels in the spiritual realm as well (it's no coincidence that the Word, and Jesus in particular, regularly referenced farming and gardening—in the agrarian society of that time, people would easily relate to the illustrations, and they naturally describe spiritual health and growth so accurately).

The 'seed' or starting point in Psalm 112 is found in verse 1: "How joyful are those who fear the Lord and delight in obeying His commands." When we plant those particular actions or intentions (mindsets, more probably), the likelihood of producing good fruit in our lives and those around us is much, much higher, than if we don't. And so, the highest quality 'seed' we can plant is a determination to honour the Lord (often mentioned in the Bible as 'fearing'), and to invest our energies in the actions that naturally go along with that determination (delighting in obedience). Just like a real crop of fruit or vegetables, there will be bumper crops and other seasons when the yield is not as high as we would like. The same is true of our lives as believers; we also have seasons of high productivity and fruitfulness, and other times when we work hard for lesser returns. The guiding principle here again, is found in verse 1: there is joy to be found in the process. That God-given, Spirit-breathed joy is sustained in good times and tough times as well. The rest of the chapter goes on to list some specifics of fruitfulness: healthy families (v2) economic provision (v3) hope and guidance (v4) confidence in God in tough times (v7,8) influence for the Kingdom (v9). The point is not to hold up a magnifying glass and scrutinize and compare our lives as to their fruitfulness, nor to become discouraged in moments when the fruit is not readily evident (seasons, remember?). The guidance and encouragement is to keep investing in good 'seed', because good seed will ultimately produce good fruit…even a 'balcony gardener' like me knows that!

APPLICATION Reflect for a few moments on the overall fruitfulness of your life. Generally speaking, and utilizing God's kindness to shape your thoughts, are you pleased with the crops that are growing? Again, remember 'seasons'. If it's applicable (in my experience, it usually is) have a conversation with the Lord about 'seed quality'; ask His assistance in both 'seeding and growing'– it's His specialty!

PRAYER

Lord, You are the master Gardener, so I put my trust in You to produce good crops in my life. Help me to regularly return to the starting point of healthy plants – the seed. Help me to plant the good seed that your Word describes: the seeds of honouring you with my whole life, and the seeds of obedience. In faith, I anticipate fruitfulness! Amen!

SIXTY-EIGHT

WORSHIP AND ADORATION

SCRIPTURE   Read Psalm 113.

OBSERVATION   No one looks up at the northern lights thinking, "Wow, I'm incredible!" What a brilliant line from Pete Greig's book "How to Pray". That line was written in reference to the act of worship and adoration, as connected to our prayer lives. The point being that when we worship God, two things generally happen: first, I get my eyes off myself, and second, I focus on God. That's in essence the sense I had as I read Psalm 113. The author drew me into an attitude of praise (v1) and giving glory (v3) to God, utilizing the mechanics of remembrance (v6-9), in order to further deepen the expression of worship, thus fortifying my faith. Can you see the pattern? I'm not sure that I know of a more effective method of getting to a healthy, close place in my relationship with God. Prayer and Bible reading are necessary, and obviously, extremely important, but there are times when those two divine disciples can potentially morph into self-focus: I bring MY needs to God in prayer, and I look for encouragement in MY life via the Word. Again, both are correct and fruit-producing principles, but conceivably self-directed. Not so with genuine worship…

APPLICATION Carve out a few moments to engage in purposeful worship today. I know, I know, in theory, our lives in totality are an act of worship (I seem to recall preaching that at some point!), but the reality of my life experience is that I have a tendency to get distracted from time to time. Setting aside a moment or two to quiet myself, look up, and praise God is a great, practical way to rediscover my spiritual equilibrium. Sometimes a sacrifice, sometimes a challenge, but always fruitful!

PRAYER

Lord, I pause even now for a moment and I praise you. Help me to remember Your Goodness and Faithfulness and to direct those remembrances back to you in praise. You are truly awesome!

Be blessed today, beloved child of God!

SIXTY-NINE

PERSPECTIVE CHANGERS

SCRIPTURE Read Psalm 114.

OBSERVATION I love moments in which I'm introduced to things that change my perspective; you know, those moments when you find yourselves saying "I had never seen it that way before!" The first three verses of Psalm 114 do exactly that. The passage begins with very familiar telling of the story of the exodus of God's people from their captivity in Egypt. Nothing that would hint of a perspective change—yet in my mind's eye, I can see the story, wonderfully, but a tad predictably, laying out before me. Then comes the curveball: "The Red Sea saw them and hurried out of their way! The water of the Jordan River turned away." (v3) I have always viewed these miraculous happenings as the Bible originally tells them: Moses raises his hand to the sea, and it splits wide open (Exodus 14), and Joshua, the priests and the Ark of the Covenant step into the river and it begins backing up (Joshua 3). Verse 3 flips things completely— no longer is the story seen from the traditional perspective of a human being's point of view; it shows the story from the water's point of view! Who knew that the sea and the river had a viewpoint? This, of course, is not entirely unknown in the Word as it relates to God's creation. All of nature is a testament to Father God's creative brilliance, and those "inanimate" objects joyfully recognize their Creator. Trees "clap their hands", as do mountains and hills (Isaiah 55:12). Floods celebrate and worship likewise (Psalm 98:8). The heavens, and the waters above them offer praise (Psalm 148:4). The stars sing for joy together (Job

38:7). Of course, Jesus noted that if human beings ceased to honour and glorify Him, the rocks would be compelled to cry out in praise (Luke 19:40)

APPLICATION So, what do we do with this little twist of perspective? I think there's a couple of things that could help us grow in strength and trust here: first, let the awe and wonder of this wash over you; that nature, in all its diversity and splendour, recognizes and worships Creator God. Every tree, every bush, every branch, every leaf, every flower, rightfully and joyfully acknowledges God! Second, if all of creation worships, and I'm part of that creation......take some time today to notice something beautiful that Father God created, and worship Him!

PRAYER

Heavenly Father, great Creator, teach me to notice your magnificence in creation. Slow me down, if You must.

Teach me to worship more fully...more naturally...more aligned, in harmony with everything else You have made...amen.

SEVENTY

SPEAK TO ME, LORD

SCRIPTURE ▶ Read Psalm 115.

OBSERVATION ▶ I don't know if you've noticed this or not, but many of these little devotional thoughts reflect the messages I am preparing in the run up to a particular Sunday. Either way, welcome to the life of a pastor! This coming Sunday's message is about hearing God; it's part of a six week series on prayer, the gist being that if the oft-repeated adage that describes prayer as a 'conversation' with God is actually true, there should be a fairly approachable pathway to the experience of hearing God's voice, in whatever form that might appear. All that to say, verses 5-7 caught my attention this morning, as I continue to ponder this most important, though sometimes confusing topic: hearing God.

Those verses describe the utter futility of simply interacting, let alone actually conversing, with an idol made by human hands (v4). The stark comparison is meant to fire both our creative imaginations, and inspire our confident trust as we anticipate that most marvellous possibility: that we, the beloved children of God, can literally hear from our Father! The man-made idol (whether shaped by actual human hands or formed by human minds) has no life, nor does it possess the capacity to create life. It cannot speak, it cannot see (v5). It can't hear or smell (v6). It does not feel anything, and it doesn't move anywhere. As if for added emphasis, the author states again "it cannot make a sound." (v7). The rest of the psalm basically recites the obvious, the absolute opposite of the lifeless idol just described. Our God, the living God, the One who helps and protects us (v10), the One who blesses and provides for us (v12,14), the One who remembers us (v12), is also the One who is alive and active, and yes, the One who listens and speaks with us! No wonder Psalm 115 ends with the hearty admonition: "Praise the Lord!"

APPLICATION Rather than list off a bunch of ways in which God can speak to us (I'll save that for Sunday!), why don't we just make this super simple? Let's just pause for a moment, take a deep breath, and in an exercise of faith and trust, say something like this:

PRAYER

Father, I thank you that your Word teaches us that You are alive, and that You lovingly speak to your children. I open my ears and my heart in anticipation of hearing from You, in whatever manner You choose to speak.

SEVENTY-ONE
DEEP EMOTIONS

SCRIPTURE ▶ Read Psalm 116.

OBSERVATION ▶ After the mentions of prayer and praying in this psalm that I referenced the other day, the next thing that jumps out at me is the broad expanse of human emotion that is on display. Now, if that's all it was, a list of emotional difficulties, that could be a tad depressing. But because it's interaction with God that is described, there's always much encouragement present.

Here's the instances of emotional expression that I noticed:

◆ (v3) troubles and sorrows
◆ (v4) grief
◆ (v8) tears and stumbling
◆ (v10) deep trouble
◆ (v11) anxiety

See what I mean about a sad list at first glance? For me, there's a couple of redeeming factors; first, I love that the Word contains such raw honesty. I think sometimes people view people of faith as emotionally shallow or dishonest, wishing difficult circumstances with nothing but a wave and a pithy quote. I can't speak for you, but that has not been the case in my life! Bringing full disclosure before the Lord is imperative; after all, He knows everything going on inside of me, right? Second, I love that for each of the items on the list, God has a response that brings hope and healing. In fact, verses 10-13 are noteworthy in that they really illustrate both points I just mentioned: "I believed in You, so I said, 'I am deeply troubled, Lord.'" Catch the order there:

> a. I believed in You,
> b. SO I said...

Our belief in Father God's unconditional love allows us to safely express our deepest concerns and troubles. That's super encouraging for me!

APPLICATION How about this for a little assignment: list each of those 'troubles' we listed earlier in one column, then, across from it in another column, write God's gracious response...

PRAYER

Simply utilize that little exercise to launch a prayer/praise time...you'll most likely find yourself repeating what the psalmist wrote in verses 16 & 17...

SEVENTY-TWO

TEACH ME TO PRAY

SCRIPTURE ▸   Read Psalm 117.

OBSERVATION ▸   This psalm is so rich, I think I'll do a couple of days' worth of devotions involving it, so just a quick heads up!

The first thing that caught my attention, again, probably because we're neck deep in a series on Prayer at Riverside (and because I'm writing this a couple of hours before I climb up on the platform to preach), are the references to prayer. In particular, the "give and take" of prayer; the two way, relational exchange that we would describe as prayer. I have often heard a phrase like "prayer is simply a conversation with God", as people try to grapple with both the simplicity and complexity of prayer; maybe you've heard that, too. I don't disagree; it's just that in my experience, that 'conversation' has often appeared a tad one-sided. Seemingly, mostly me talking, not as much God responding. This psalm contains some beautiful reminders and examples of the 'dialogue.' Verses 1&2 both reference a response-filled interaction: God "hears my voice" and also "bends down to listen." Other translations render that as "inclined His ear", which elevates God's response even further, inferring an act similar to a taller adult to a smaller child, kneeling down and cupping the ear to ensure that every word is caught, every nuance understood. Similarly, verse 4 "I called on the name of the Lord", verse 11 "I cried out to you", and verse 17 "I offer you a sacrifice of thanksgiving and call on your name", all express the act of praying, and all subsequently record the responsive heart and ear of our Heavenly Father.

APPLICATION ▶ All that (and a full month of preaching and teaching at Riverside!) for what exactly? Personally, I have certainly felt a new sense of urgency from the Lord, with regards to prayer. Hopefully, we don't fall into old patterns of complacency—lots of hearing, but often not much doing (James 1:22). As the first disciples once entreated Jesus: "Lord, teach us to pray". I believe that He has always been willing to do just that, and He continues to be willing. The only real question to be considered is "when do I start?" He will be faithful to guide you into the "conversation".

PRAYER

Uhmm…I guess this is as good as anything else:

Teach me to pray…. I'm here, ready to listen and learn.

SEVENTY-THREE

UNFAILING LOVE

SCRIPTURE   Read Psalm 117.

OBSERVATION   A couple of initial thoughts about Psalm 117: first, it is the shortest chapter in the Bible, and second, because it's so short, it's possible to breeze past it as though it's more of a footnote than anything else! That's kind of what I found myself doing this morning, perhaps preparing myself for the rigours of the longest chapter (Psalm 119) that lays just ahead. This chapter largely contains two main points, which are actually one continuous thought: an invitation and encouragement to praise the Lord, followed by a reminder as to why that is an appropriate and faith-building investment.

And so, we praise (v1). We praise when things go well; we praise when things go sideways. That singular discipline is one of the keys to Christian living. It is not simply the "power of positive thinking", as some have erroneously labelled it. They are the faith-building, life-sustaining, God-honouring, biblically-aligning utterances that grow deep roots and provide strength and courage for life and living! From there, we go to the fuel for praise, which is God's unfailing love towards us, and remembering His faithfulness (v2). If all you could muster in a difficult moment was a reciting of that one verse, inserting your name and making it personal, I think you'd probably find yourself able to navigate the storm. Praise is a remarkable and powerful thing: never forget, praise is gift and a weapon for our benefit, far more than it is for God!

APPLICATION ▶   Pause for a moment and praise the Lord, regardless of your current situation, maybe even in spite of your current situation. Fuel your praise by remembering actual instances where God has been faithful. As we sing sometimes: "If He (God) has done it before, He can do it again!"

PRAYER ▶

Thank you, Lord, for your unfailing love toward me, for the way You have faithfully stayed by my side, even in moments where I have felt abandoned. I know that You will never leave! I pray today for the courage and insight to continue to praise You, in faith and growing hope of your deliverance and provision. Amen. So be it.

SEVENTY-FOUR

TRUSTING GOD

SCRIPTURE ▶ Read Psalm 118.

OBSERVATION ▶ This past Sunday, we celebrated our 10 year anniversary at the church that we have the privilege of pastoring. My contribution to the festivities was to preach—no big surprise there! I bring that up only to highlight a certain process or discipline that resides in a preacher's world, one that I found myself utilizing as I ponder Psalm 118 this morning, and that I used multiple times in preparing the message that I brought to the church yesterday. And that process is: simplification. In other words, distilling down a lot of information into as simple a form as possible, for ease of communication, understanding, and memory.

The message I delivered from Ezekiel 47:1-12, took several weeks and numerous re-writes to get to its final, simplified form; literally a journey from several broad concepts to just three words (the three words happen to be: Design, Depth, and Destiny).

I felt a similar, recognizable sense with regards to this particular passage. Psalm 118 is an expansive passage; it covers many themes, from several different vantage points, and like many other psalms, it covers a wide variety of experiences and emotions. All of these things are noteworthy and potentially helpful, but sometimes a little daunting to approach, as it's tough to settle on a concentrated, singular theme. That's perfectly fine, of course, and there are times in which I find that a longish, wide-ranging discourse is very soothing to my inner being. But, being a simple man, who tends to thrive on simplicity and ease of understanding, let me be so bold as to distill this psalm down to one thought, captured in verses 8&9: "It is better to take refuge in the Lord than to trust in princes." That's the touch point for me. Learning, practicing, re-learning, re-practicing, the simple art of trusting God. As the psalmist rightly notes; both people (in many ways, shapes and forms, in person and from a distance, and, in the interest of honesty, I must also apply this to myself) and princes (authority figures and structures, human leadership, governments and organizations) will disappoint us and fail, but the Lord will never do so!

APPLICATION Find a way, or ways, to develop your trust in the Lord; as the scripture said, to "take refuge" in Him. How you do that may look different to you than it does for me, but that really is simply an aside. Don't get distracted or discouraged by that.

It's such a beautiful and personal thing, that I hesitate to say "do this, or do that" in order to discover the joy and truth of the principle. Perhaps you're already practicing the single greatest 'method' of growing a deepening reliance on the Lord: taking a few moments to spend time with Him in the Word...

PRAYER

Lord, as the world swirls and churns around me, help me to snuggle up close to You. Teach me to trust, and to find refuge and security in You. Help me to discover the peace and rest that You promise. Amen.

SEVENTY-FIVE

GOD'S AUTHORITY

SCRIPTURE ▶ Read Psalm 118.

OBSERVATION ▶ I'd like to take a moment to step into one more observation I noticed in Psalm 118; this is as much for me as it is for anyone else, for in truth, it's something that I don't understand terribly well. The passage I reference is found in verses 10-12, and has to do with the concept and principle of "the authority of the Lord".

Three times the author states, in the context of fierce battle with his enemies, that he was able to overcome these adversaries with that particular dynamic force. What did he mean exactly? How was this weapon utilized? And for us today, how can we access this same truth when we encounter situations that seem to require a 'warfare' response? Honestly, those questions remain somewhat unclear for me. I'm mature enough in my faith to know that there are no 'magic wand' solutions to challenging life circumstances, but I'm still struck with a sense of significance regarding this 'authority' principle. So, let's start with what I do know for certain (it's a fairly short list, I assure you!):

- ◆ God is all powerful
- ◆ I am not
- ◆ There is something steadying and stabilizing (even 'attack-oriented', if you will), that happens in me when I align myself with the authority of God through His Word.

Mark 4:9 quotes Jesus as saying it this way: "Anyone with ears to hear should listen and understand." The word 'understand' literally means to 'stand-under'; to yield to; to get in line with; to align with. In other words, the faith-building practicality of 'standing under' God's authority is simply that: a confession or declaration of alignment that produces a confident trust moving forward into the battlegrounds of my life. Familiarity with the Word is obviously a huge help in this regard. Knowing what God says, knowing who He is via a close relationship, and linking those two concepts through prayer, worship and praise, and meditative time in the Word, in very practical terms allow for a growing embrace and personal experience of what is ultimately manifested in our lives by 'the authority of the Lord'. A simple reminder: it's HIS authority and MY submission that ultimately enable confidence—inspiring trust to grow!

APPLICATION Even though some of these spiritual principles are vast, and perhaps a little hard to pin down, they are still valid, accessible and approachable; otherwise, they wouldn't be there in the first place. So, here's my application for today, and it will come in the form of a....

PRAYER

Heavenly Father; You are all powerful, I am not. You have never lost a battle, and you never will, including the battles that may be raging in my life right now. Grant me the grace and wisdom to align myself with you, with your authority, though I may not fully understand everything going on around me. And teach me to rest in your loving care. Amen.

Thanks for listening in to my heart, as I, like you, continue to journey forward...

SEVENTY-SIX

MATURING OUR FAITH

SCRIPTURE ▶   Read Psalm 119:1-8.

OBSERVATION ▶   Okay, so right off the top, Psalm 119 is a long chunk of scripture; but don't let that put you off. It was originally written as an acrostic poem, divided into 22 sections of 8 verses each; there's a few other poetic tidbits included, like that each 8 verse stanza begins with a successive letter of the Hebrew alphabet, but that's really just a further nod to its beauty, brilliance and design!   For our purposes, we'll simply navigate its depths, one eight verse chunk or so at a time…starting with verses 1-8. This passage is rich in dark green highlights in my Bible. Dark green is the pencil crayon colour I use to denote the actions of faith, choices of faith, and lifestyle of a faith-follower of God—you can view the little colour coding guide at the front of this book. To some, I suppose, this might come across as excessively demanding: a type of "do this, do that" kind of message. Personally, I don't see it that way; I find it encouraging and helpful. It gives me some guardrails for living; a target, a measuring stick, a standard to hold up. Verse 6 actually says as much: "…when I compare my life with your commands." It's important to remember that this 'comparing' is not with others—that's a huge mistake that we make sometimes, and it invariably leads to faulty, usually punitive, often discouraging conclusions—certainly never the intent of God's Word! I guess it also resonated in me because (here comes the pastor in me again!) I'm in the middle of preparing a series on Riverside's DNA. In other words, the passing down, both intentional and unintentional, from one person to another, of the godly design, heritage and blessing of God. The basis of that series is returning to re-read a pledge that Ingrid and I made ten years ago at the birth of Riverside. In effect, a 'comparing' of our lives with the direction we felt God had given us for this particular body of believers under our care. What a great, sometimes stretching exercise! What strength, comfort and fruitfulness come from simply making inner determinations to walk with the Lord (v3).

APPLICATION I know I can't speak for you, but my response to this passage is pretty straightforward: re-dedicate, re-commit, re-align myself to walking this out in my life. Thankfully, a maturing faith and friendship with the Lord has taught me to waste as little time as possible with regret over the times that I have wandered off the path. After all, He's not grinding me over it, is He? He simply and kindly picks me up, brushes me off, and gently points me back in the right direction.

PRAYER

Father God, thank you for caring enough to provide guidelines and guardrails for our lives. Lord, we both know that I don't always get it right. Help me to focus on you, to experience your forgiveness and grace, as I re-state my intentions to walk out "consistent actions that reflect your decrees." (v5). Thank you for tenderly guiding our lives… I love you, Father!

SEVENTY-SEVEN

INTENTIONALITY, AGAIN!

SCRIPTURE   Read Psalm 108 :9-16.

OBSERVATION   I happen to be up very early this morning, even by my 'old man' standards! Part of it is excitement I feel in anticipation of our men's BBQ later today, and the opportunity to impart life and vitality to a group of men; the other part is simply the knowledge that overall, I have a very busy day that needs to be approached with intentionality, in order to accomplish and fulfill responsibilities, expectations and goals. Which is exactly what struck me in my devotions this morning, as I read and pondered verses 9-16 of this psalm: the idea, and the actions, of 'intentionality'. Scan the passage and note how frequently the author makes an "I have" or an "I will" statement.

- v10: "I have tried hard to find you…"
- v11: "I have hidden your word in my heart…"
- v13: "I have recited aloud all the regulations…"
- v14: "I have rejoiced in your laws…"
- v15: "I will study your commandments…"
- v16: "I will delight in your decrees…"

And that's not to mention four other purposeful actions not prefaced by "I have" or I will"! (v 12 "I praise", v 12 "teach me", v 15 "I reflect ", v 16 "I will not forget")

I don't remember a lot from my teenage years, but I do recall an unnamed teacher solemnly intoning in some high school class somewhere, "If you fail to plan, you plan to fail." Most of us have heard some form of that truism at some point in our lives; having heard it repetitively doesn't lessen its truth, and healthy spirituality is no exception. The psalmist got it. Approaching our relationship with God contains a healthy dose of purpose. Nothing terribly complicated there. So, why do we so often struggle with inconsistency and following through on our sincere intentions? I suppose it's nothing more than being human and failing to harness the power of intentionality—we all struggle with it in varying degrees, from time to time.

APPLICATION   So, what to do about it? At the risk of sounding like our friend, Captain Obvious, be intentional! Like any habit-forming behaviour, thoughtfully and purposefully approaching this is key; the psalmist recorded his method of developing intentionality a couple of thousand years ago, don't forget—as far as human nature goes, not that much has changed!

PRAYER

Read today's passage again, with intention.

Pray today's passage again, with intention.

SEVENTY-EIGHT

HELP US TO UNDERSTAND

SCRIPTURE Read Psalm 119:17-32.

OBSERVATION I love it when ideas or truths are presented with the help of "bookends". Such is the case with today's devotional thought, to the point that it's actually the bookends themselves that caught my heart's attention. Let me explain further: first the concept of the "bookend", then the over-arching thought being put forward.

In my eyes, verses 18 and 32 are the two linked ideas (you'll note that we're actually covering two 8 verse stanzas today, not the usual one). Verse 8 says: "Open my eyes to see the wonderful truths in your instructions." Verse 32 says virtually the same thing using these words: "I will pursue your commands, for you expand my understanding." Both passages contain these similar, united thoughts, for our purposes, the "bookends".

   a. I need your help, Lord, to grasp, understand and implement your Word, your Truth, in my life, and,

   b. I will do my part in the process.

Next, the over-arching thought: Both of those realities are vital to growing as a follower of God and a student of His Word. Each of those concepts, taken on their own, won't quite get the job done, will they? I most definitely need the Lord's assistance in understanding the vastness and power of the Word (He ultimately inspired and 'authored' it, right?), but without the regular discipline of carving out time and space to seek out that assistance…well, I think you get the point; especially poignant as you join me today in sharing this devotional! The rest of the verses in between just relate the challenges and realities of life as we try to work out the partnership we share with the Lord.

APPLICATION What simplicity and comfort are present in this passage and its construction! Lord, I need help to understand, in order to learn and grow in my faith. And, give me a heart that is committed to the joy (note: not just the discipline…) of seeking You in Your Word. What a great directive to continue putting down deep roots in the Lord (some of you might recognize Jeremiah 17:8 here)…

PRAYER

Simple enough: Personalize the "bookends" as your prayer….

SEVENTY-NINE

LOVING THE WORD

SCRIPTURE   Read Psalm 119:33-40.

OBSERVATION   One of the recurring themes through this entire lengthy psalm is the psalmist's love for the "Word"; put another way, his dependence on it, his affection for it, his searching of it, his hunger to be taught and guided through it. He regularly references its influence in his life, as well as his active response to it. Verse 37 is one of many such mentions of the "Word", and it contains a truly wonderful insight into what God's Word can produce in an individual: "...give me life through your Word." So, the author expresses a conviction of what the Bible is capable of doing, and also what he is longing for the Word to accomplish in his life: give life! The likelihood of that actually happening is quite naturally increased by the frequency of which someone makes themselves available to that reality. Now, without a doubt, the Word is powerful enough to radically change a life with a single mention, but it makes sense that repeated, regular, and heartfelt time spent developing a rich devotional life holds a higher degree of probability in that regard. I really love the way that Isaiah 55:11 puts it: "It is the same with my Word. I send it out, and it always produces fruit. It will accomplish all I want it to, and it will prosper everywhere I send it." Wow! That is really an amazing revelation, when we view the power of the Word, as described by God Himself!

APPLICATION ▶ Okay, this is probably going to sound pretty lame, but here goes: Spend time in the Word! I know that there are many reasons why folks find this challenging, and each of those reasons carry varying degrees of validity (I'm not being dismissive, but I'm not going to get into those right now). All I can tell you is this, from my own experience as a follower of God, far more than as a Pastor (that's another discussion for another day!), my life has experienced the "life" that we referenced back at the start of this devotional, in more ways than I could adequately describe. It would be appropriate here, to echo something we say at Riverside every single Sunday morning: "This is my Bible; it is God speaking to me…"

PRAYER ▶

The psalmist of old said it best:

"…give me life through your word." So be it.

EIGHTY

HIS MIGHTY POWER AT WORK

SCRIPTURE ▶ Read Psalm 119:41-72.

OBSERVATION ▶ I recognize that this passage is a little longer than the more typical eight verse chunk that we started with, but as I read and pondered the Word, I noted a connection that fell within that span of verses. That note was this: there's simply too much wonderful stuff to choose from! We could easily settle here for an extended period of time, which we might actually do— stay tuned! Okay, enough said about that. To the Word!

We talked about proportionality a while back, specifically from Psalm 90; the idea being that God, who knows no limitations, liberally pours into the lives of his children, who really know and experience nothing but human limitations. This can be jarring initially, but incredibly freeing as we continuously bump into this truth: His proportions are never our proportions! (Psalm 90:15) Today's verses communicate a similar theme, this time in reference to promise-making and promise-keeping. While this is not meant to be an exact science or calculation, it is definitely meant to be faith-building and encouraging.

Here are the listed instances as they appear, followed by a note of who is doing the promising. (I think the ratio works out to about 3-1, just so you know…)

- ◆ **v41**: "...the salvation that You promised me." (GOD)
- ◆ **v49**: "Remember Your promise to me; it is my only hope." (GOD)
- ◆ **v50**: "Your promise revives me; it comforts me in all my troubles." (GOD)
- ◆ **v57**: "I promise to obey your words!" (ME)
- ◆ **v65**: "You have done many good things for me, Lord, just as You have promised." (GOD)

Actually, turns out that it was 4-1, but who's counting? The point is this: God ALWAYS gives more to us than we could give to Him! Whatever we humanly promise to do for Him (and regularly fail, I might add), He does far, far more to and for us (and never fails). Ephesians 3:20 says it this way: "Now all glory to God, who is able, through His mighty power at work within us, to accomplish infinitely more than we might ask or think." I think the word "infinitely" makes my point about God's views on proportionality!

APPLICATION   Ponder that for a moment—don't hurry past that. Perhaps that is the best application of all…allow yourself to get lost momentarily in that magnificent thought…apply that as a faith-builder as you might approach the various challenges that your life presents…envision how much bigger, more generous, more faithful, more kind, more wise, more every good thing God is, in comparison to our humanness…

PRAYER

Simply and confidently pray Ephesians 3:20… Amen. A quick shout out to the faithful men who gathered to pray at 4pm today— wow! THAT was powerful! Blessings, dear friends…

EIGHTY-ONE

NIGHT THOUGHTS

SCRIPTURE ▶ Read Psalm 119:41-72.

OBSERVATION ▶ I had a vivid dream last night. Now, the point of telling you that is not that I had a vivid dream last night. I mention it because of something I noted, and have been pondering, in the passage we've been lingering in for the past couple of days. Accordingly, I've called this devotional "Night Thoughts". Verses 55 and 62 both reference instances in which the psalmist interacts with God at night:

- ◆ "I reflect at night" (v55)
- ◆ "I rise at midnight to thank You…" (v62)

In reading the rest of the passage surrounding those verses, one can easily imagine many of the other interactions taking place at night. That certainly has been my experience. I am a very light sleeper, and therefore wake up frequently each and every night.

What comfort and rest are produced when my thoughts instinctively go to the Lord. Less time worrying, more time praying and worshipping, and consequently growing my 'faith roots' deeper! As I have disciplined myself to do this through the years, it has literally become instinctive. I wake up, I seek the Lord through prayer, I thank Him in praise, I remember answered prayers, I sing a few notes of a worship song (in my head, so as not to disturb Ingrid)…and sometimes I recall a vivid dream that God has given me... the length of time I stay awake no longer becomes a cause for stress or anxiety—it simply means more conscious time with the Lord. By the way, the Psalms are quite regular in their mention of other "night thoughts": Check out Psalm 1:2, 3:5, 4:4, 4:8, 5:3, 6:6, just as a start.

APPLICATION   I'm not trying to play amateur psychologist here, to analyze your fears and correct your sleep patterns, and to present these observations as a cure-all. I'm simply sharing with you what I have experienced and discovered over many years of purposefully developing a heart after God. For me, it really is a delightful thing, a supremely comforting thing; to awaken at night, whether it's for a few seconds, or for an extended period, and naturally fall into rhythmic step with Jesus...

PRAYER

Lord, you know my thoughts, my concerns, the things that I worry about. Teach me to use the night as an opportunity to grow my trust in you, through loving friendship; help me to commit my cares to You, knowing that You are more than able to carry them. (1 Peter 5:7) Amen.

EIGHTY-TWO

GIVE ME THE SENSE

SCRIPTURE ▶ Read Psalm 119:73-80.

OBSERVATION ▶ The Bible is generally not described as a "humorous" book; there are, however, moments that show up on occasion that certainly can bring a smile or even a chuckle. This happened for me this morning… Verse 73 reads: "You made me; You created me. Now give me the sense to follow your commands." (Other translations tend toward a less 'funny' approach, more along the lines of "increase my understanding.") For our purposes, I'm sticking with "give me the sense"! A quick reminder: we're using the New Living Translation (unless noted otherwise.) Upon viewing other people's lives (especially doable these days via YouTube etc), we can often find ourselves wondering: "What on earth were they thinking?" Now, I know God doesn't think like us human beings, but I can't help but wonder if, even for the briefest of moments, He ever wonders something similar? With full and easy access to the mind of God through the Word, complete with its bounty of promises, with the literal indwelt presence of the Holy Spirit (I speak of a born again individual here), and with the capacity to have made repetitive mistakes in the past and to have been patiently and lovingly instructed by God to learn from them, how on earth do we lack the sense to consistently follow God and obey His commands? Pretty astonishing when you phrase it that way, isn't it? And yet, the age-old experience is uttered by the psalmist: I lack the sense to follow you to the degree that You deserve, Lord; and to the degree that produces the most solidly predictable life results. As we used to say, "Been there, done that." Moving forward, I really like the author's approach to this very human dilemma, and I think it's critical, lest we find ourselves mired in despondency and harsh self-criticism. He dusts himself off, and almost immediately gets back to upholding and embracing the truth and hope of the Word! Literally, every successive verse in this stanza (v 74-80) brings the same directive: get back to the truth of the Word (described as "the Word", "your regulations", "promises", "your instructions", "commandments", "your laws", "your decrees") and experience its restorative power. In other words, don't linger on your failures, your moments of "lacking sense"; keep on keeping on, learning and trusting as you go...

APPLICATION If you haven't already done something like this, perhaps it's a good time to consider it: make a commitment to regular, unhurried time in the Word. Various times and demands of life can make this challenging for sure, but as the saying goes "we've all got 24 hours in a day..."

PRAYER

Lord, You made me; You created me. Now give me the sense to follow your commands. Amen.

EIGHTY-THREE

REMINDING & REMEMBERING

SCRIPTURE ▸ Read Psalm 119:81-88.

OBSERVATION ▸ Every now and then I find myself a little tired. I think that's common to us all. Reading this passage reminded me of that reality, and provided a couple of helpful insights into navigating times of weariness. First, verse 82 popped for me: "My eyes are straining to see your promises come true." What a perfect description of how I feel about certain areas of my life that are, humanly speaking, unfinished. Inwardly, my spiritual man "strains" to see God complete the things that He has promised by His Word. This is nothing more than a faith exercise, and is common to every believer. My encouragement to you? Keep looking, keep hoping, keep trusting…God is faithful to keep His Promise!

Next, in the midst of the language of the tiring journey the psalmist is on, he reminds himself (and us today) of the trustworthiness of God's Word. This is a simple, repetitive theme of the entire Bible: we can trust in God and His Word. Let me re-phrase that: we MUST trust in God and His Word! Dear friend, at the end of the day, it's all we've got, and it's all we need. Matthew 24:35 tells us "Heaven and earth will disappear, but my words will never disappear." Be strengthened today by turning to God's Word!

Finally, the author turns to this supreme truth, in verse 88:

God's unfailing love! It's quite astonishing how quickly we can forget this and succumb to the discouragement of the world's messaging. I don't say that with any hint of accusation or condemnation. I am simply taking a glance at my own experience. In times of intense pressure, or even in times of mild discomfort, remembering the simplest yet profound truth of all is a powerful remedy: we are loved by God!

APPLICATION ▸   I guess we're asking for a spiritual "assist" here: nothing we spoke of today is new. And yet, we're asking Holy Spirit to help us remember; to remind us; to spend less time being consumed by situations around us, and to move more quickly into embracing truth via the Word of God!

PRAYER

Lord, please extend your Grace through the act of reminding me. Help us to remember well!

EIGHTY-FOUR
TIMELESSNESS

SCRIPTURE Read Psalm 119:89-96.

OBSERVATION When I was young, and beginning my journey to establish the Word as the foundation of my life, I would hear people say things like: "Reading the Bible is just like reading the newspaper of the day". They inferred that the Word timelessly addresses the condition of the world, as well as the condition of the human heart, in a way that offers the reader insight, stability, direction, and comfort. While I probably didn't fully understand what those folks meant back then (and I certainly wouldn't call myself an expert on prophecy as it pertains to these most interesting days and times), I would declare that the Word remains secure and dependable in its ability to provide what a modern-day disciple needs to thrive and flourish! Take Psalm 119: 89-91, for example. I noted three rapid-fire, faith-building truths that lifted my spirit as I read them this morning:

- God's eternal word stands firm (v89); that's a two-fold statement of promise! First, the Word is eternal-it never changes, diminishes or falters. Second, it stands firm in heaven. Is there anything in all of creation more trustworthy than that?
- God's faithfulness extends to every generation (v90). That means that the same immovable, unshakable, everlasting characteristics that described God way back in Bible times, apply to me today, and apply to every generation that follows! Some folks consider the Bible to be outdated and irrelevant.

The Word itself begs to differ!

◆ Everything serves His plans (v91). That's really important to remember right now, in light of a chaotic, unpredictable, sometimes frightening world around us. Nothing happens outside of God's knowledge, indeed, His plans! More than that; world events actually SERVE His plans!

APPLICATION ▶ The Word often encourages us to comfort ourselves with thoughts like these. So, let's do just that. Slowly re-read this portion of Psalm 119, especially verses 89-91. Pause after each individual verse. Close your eyes and meditate on that truth. Let it wash over you. Let it penetrate deep into your heart and mind…

PRAYER ▶

Simply and thoughtfully recite today's portion of the Word; offer it up to the Lord as your prayer.

EIGHTY-FIVE
VOWS & PROMISES

SCRIPTURE Read Psalm 119:105-112.

OBSERVATION I recently attended a wedding. That is not unusual in itself, and I suspect that as a pastor, I have probably attended more of these events than most!

The wedding itself is not the point; it's the vows that I want to focus on. Vows, and the deep commitment behind them, are increasingly rare to find. I actually counsel couples who are preparing to write their own vows for their wedding ceremony to stop and consider the solemn gravity of a vow. Many have started to compose their vows, only to discover that what they are reciting is much more akin to a "gee, I think you're swell" sentiment; which is appropriate at a wedding, but is most certainly not a 'vow'. A vow speaks of a promise, or a sacrificial dedication, if necessary; an unwavering commitment to keeping the vow or promise made. The biblical term 'covenant' probably best encapsulates the intent and its execution. The psalmist makes this statement in verse 106: "I've promised it once, and I'll promise it again: I will obey your regulations."

Now, to whom is the author making this promise? To the Lord, the ultimate source of the Word. Here's an important understanding concerning promises made to God: because God takes the promises He makes very, very seriously, and has every intent on following through with them (the book of Isaiah is particularly full of examples; see 9:6&7, 14:24, 34:16, 42: 8&9,

to list a few), He seems to expect His children and the ones who make promises to Him, to do the same! This is simply a truism for being a follower of God. It is not meant to heap guilt upon us when we as humans don't follow through with our commitments to God, nor is it intended to drive us harder towards proving our love of God through our own efforts. Praise God for Grace! Rather, like the psalmist said, it's good to re-visit the commitments we make to the Lord, whether they are made in good times or tough times, and double down in our efforts to fulfill our vows. Very similar to a married couple refreshing their commitment to their relationship through various means, romantic or practical, in words and in actions.

APPLICATION ▶   What promises have you made to God? In today's passage, the psalmist promised to obey God's Word. Personally, I have promised many things through the years, not always successfully: to regularly read the Word, to pray more frequently, to give faithfully from my income, to serve God with my whole heart, and to be more patient with people, to name a few. The point is not to belabour the failures; it is rather to encourage a remembrance, a new embrace, to anticipate learning through missteps that produce a deeper level of commitment, and then by extension, a deeper level of fulfillment and joy. Perhaps today is a good day for you to reinvestigate the commitments you have made to the Lord. You can be assured that He waits patiently and tenderly for that honest conversation, in order to fully restore you and grant you the strength to fulfill your vows!

PRAYER

Lord, thank you for your grace. Thank you that I will always find a compassionate welcome when I approach You. Please give me the wisdom, perseverance and strength to follow through on my promises to You. I look forward to seeing Your promises fulfilled in my life, as well as experiencing the deep satisfaction and fruitfulness of fulfilling my promises to You. Amen.

Bless you, dear friends...

EIGHTY-SIX

DETERMINATION

SCRIPTURE ▶ Read Psalm 119:105-112.

OBSERVATION ▶ At the end of our All Church Prayer meeting recently, a young lady who attends our church timidly spoke up as we were all getting up to go. She said she had something to share with the group, which the Lord had impressed on her heart as the meeting had gone on. She then shared a vivid picture of a person wading through a turbulent stretch of a river. The emphasis, she felt, was the sense of determination that was etched on the face of the individual who was crossing the river. Determination to make it across, determination to successfully complete the crossing; a sharp focus on the task that still awaited on the other side. Her picture captured my attention for another reason; it was because of the repetitive use of a certain word or concept, which is used again in today's devotional. "I am determined to keep your decrees to the very end." says Psalm 119:112.

There was that word again: "determination". Just to complete the story, I had bumped into that concept while spending time with the young men of our Quest men's team, as we searched the Word for a sense of direction and identity. It showed up in Isaiah 50:7: "I have set my face like a stone, determined to do His will." For me, God often speaks via repetition. I don't think that I'm necessarily a slow learner, but I am human, and often fail to catch things that are significant the first time around—I need to be graciously reminded, to have things underlined and then patiently explained by a loving Father. So, there it was: determination, three times in quick succession. Discussions of spiritual growth aside, there is something simple, yet powerful, in making an inner determination about something. It may not sound terribly profound, or even deeply spiritual, but it is unmistakably present in the life of a follower of God. I doubt that any truly mature believer has arrived where they are without it. There are even times when it may feel like that's all you've got to propel you forward. A deep inner commitment to finish the journey of faith; to see God's promises realized; to experience what we have hoped for. In the simplest of terms, that's really what our faith-journeys are: an unshakable determination to partner with God by faith, to see us through the sometimes raging rivers of life, to safety on the other side. Here's the scripture the precious young lady shared along with the picture she had: "When you go through deep waters, I will be with you. When you go through rivers of difficulty, you will not drown." (Isaiah 43:2a) What a hope and promise we have from God, through His Word!

APPLICATION I'm not really even sure as to how to proceed here. The need for determination is not very glamorous, nor is it necessarily achieved in a single moment. It usually comes through failures and doubts; the honest stuff that we all experience as followers of God. I suppose it is actually a series of "re-determinations"; asking the Father of Grace, to patiently explain it again and again, and to grant us the courage and strength to keep moving towards the other shore. As the psalmist wrote: "I am determined…"

PRAYER

Lord, we need your help to navigate life; to not lose hope; to keep moving forward in faith. Teach us to trust You more fully. Thank you for developing the powerful, practical, spiritual discipline of determination in us, your children. Amen.

Bless you, dear friends…

EIGHTY-SEVEN

HUMBLE SERVANTS

SCRIPTURE ▶   Read Psalm 119:121-128.

OBSERVATION ▶   My wife, Ingrid, has always had a fondness for British television shows, the ones typically found on PBS-type networks. Most recently, she has been really smitten with Downton Abbey; it's particular time period, it's quirky (to us in North America, anyway!) cultural norms, it's social comment on class structures, and of course, it's gentle, though often biting, humour. Today's passage reminded me of that, with its references to 'servants' (v 124, 125). The concept of servants and masters is largely unfamiliar to modern folks, though it was an everyday experience and observation in the time in which the Bible was written—there are even specific passages written directly to slaves and servants, who also happened to be followers of Jesus. (see Ephesians 6:5-8 and Colossians 3:22-4:1, for example) All that to say that it's a difficult concept for most modern readers to envision, or to see themselves as part of a relevant expression. And yet, the master/servant picture is fairly common to biblical literature, especially as it relates to a believer's posture and position in Christ. Both the gospels and Paul's writings use the terminology; in fact, Paul actually refers to himself as "a slave of Christ." (Romans 1:1) So, what do we do with all of this servant/slave talk? How does it apply to our lives today?

I think it begins with an inner posture towards the Lord; for me, the act of worship is very helpful in this regard. Any expression that places me in a "less than" position is beneficial. That's not to say downtrodden or belittled—that's certainly not Jesus' attitude toward me! Maybe John the Baptist said it best in John 3:30: "He must become greater and greater, and I must become less and less."

APPLICATION Try to take on that "less than" mindset. Humbly utilize worship (and its attendant postures—raising hands, kneeling, speaking praise and honour to the Lord...) to your benefit. When we are able to see God as "more than", it tends to bring with it a healthy perspective and understanding of faith and trust; a loving, caring Master, who kindly and generously tends to the needs of His servants.

PRAYER

Lord, Master; I humbly submit to Your loving care. I pray for wisdom and humility in my approach to You. Grow in me a deepening trust in Your goodness. Help me to rest in Your love today. Your servant, Terry (place your name here, if you'd like...) Amen. So be it.

EIGHTY-EIGHT

THE PROMISER

SCRIPTURE ▶ Read Psalm 119:137-144.

OBSERVATION ▶

A spiritual leadership principle that I learned early on in my ministry career is this: You can't lead anyone to a place you have not been yourself. In other words, I can't legitimately teach people about something like having faith, notably a deep faith, if I haven't gone through the life experiences and related faith exercises that produce deep and abiding faith. That's a sobering reality, knowing what we know about what goes into the development of a deeply-rooted faith system.

This portion of Psalm 119 demonstrates that principle, in order to grow our confidence and dependence in the One who ultimately produces spiritual results, be it faith, trust, or any other healthy expression of spirituality. There are two entities being tested in this passage: God Himself (v140), and the psalmist (v143), who represents us in the illustration. First to God: The Word says "Your promises have been thoroughly tested…" This testing has been at the hands of countless followers of God throughout the ages. Person after person, in story after story, in crisis after crisis, have held on to God's promises (you probably find yourself doing exactly that right now, in one way or another) and proven them to be utterly trustworthy and dependable. The Bible is full of instances in which God publicly declares a promise, oftentimes audacious, and then invites human beings to participate with Him in the fulfilling of that promise. Titus 1:2 says it like this: "God—who does not lie-promised them before the world began." Whether the promise concerns eternal life, as it does in Titus, or concerns a promise for provision, protection, wisdom, restoration (or whatever you happen to be believing God for), the principle is established: His promises have been thoroughly tested, and proven true. This then allows the psalmist to personally lean into God's promises (or 'commands', as used here) for hope, strength, and comfort, during times of "pressure and stress" (v143). Because God's words have been successfully tried and tested, by natural extension, we can confidently move ahead in faith as well, knowing that His words will not fail us. God leads us forward in faith, to places that He Himself, as the author and finisher of faith, has already been!

APPLICATION I normally don't recommend doing this, but I think it works in this case. Track down a list of God's promises; they can sometimes be listed in the back pages of certain Bibles, or in the form of a booklet. Certainly a quick internet search would reveal some. Once you find a list, slowly and prayerfully review those promises; ponder the wonder of the Promiser.

Ponder the wonder of all the lives that have read those exact words, holding on to the words of the One who never fails…

PRAYER

Talk to God about His promises. Ask Him to direct you to the places that you need to focus on, the specific promises you need to cling to. Personally, I have found many times that a single promise has sustained me through decades of my journey; I think a deep, intimate conversation with God, based on one faith-principle, is probably more effective ultimately, than a lengthy list… But that may just be me!

Be blessed by the Promiser, dear friends…

EIGHTY-NINE
AGAIN, THE WORD

SCRIPTURE ▶ Read Psalm 119:145-152.

OBSERVATION ▶ For this devotional, I think we'll just meander through this passage, pausing along the way for a few brief moments. The common themes throughout the stanza are the references to the Word of God (decrees, laws, words, promise, regulations, instructions, commands), and the author's intentional, zealous approach to God's words. Verse 145 begins with an almost shocking ferocity "answer me, Lord!" I have always appreciated the honesty of the Psalms. A good reminder here: one of the main reasons we pray is for answers from God, right? Verse 146 presents a really interesting perspective again on why we pray, this time from a different angle altogether "Rescue me, that I may obey." Not only do we pray in order to receive something from God, we also pray in order to give back our obedience and love—that's worthy of a little more thought.

Verse 147 stresses the importance of putting our hope in the Word of God, and ultimately, in the God of the Word! Verse 148 describes my own experience of sleeping and waking very well: the more years that I have invested in study of the Bible, the more naturally His promises come to mind as I occasionally find myself staring at the ceiling in the middle of the night! Verse 149 reminds us of the faithful love of God, and uses a word that we haven't seen much before: "revived". What a beautiful and powerful combination of spiritual concepts: faithful love and personal revival! Verse 150 describes the very unfair and painful experience that the author is undergoing. Verse 151 reiterates the importance of remembering the nearness of God. Written in the time of the Old Covenant, this was a much more challenging exercise than it is for today's New Covenant believer; still, continuously reminding ourselves of this truth should be a regular part of our prayer lives, our worship, our Bible reading… Verse 152 is an acknowledgment of many years of investing in the hungry pursuit of the Word. Don't be discouraged if you don't have that personal history to draw on yet. The fact that you're here today is another step in building that beautiful reality and familiarity!

APPLICATION For this, we could simply re-read the entire portion, 145-152. Insert your name and story into every verse, line by line. Ponder each statement, each truth, and each application as you go…

PRAYER

Same as above, I think. Blessings, dear friends…

NINETY
A DISCERNING MIND

SCRIPTURE ▶   Read Psalm 119:169-176.

OBSERVATION ▶   Like several previous portions of this psalm, I think we'll pause for a couple of visits. Again, there's simply too much good stuff to cover in one reading! It was the very first verse (v169), right out of the gate that caught my attention, and made me pause and reflect; from that pause, I found my mind running through several cross-references that augmented the same thought, that I'll share later in this devotional. "O Lord, listen to my cry; give me the discerning mind You promised." (v169) A couple of quick observations, then the cross-references:

"…listen to my cry…" I don't keep statistics on this, but the number of people I connect with that are finding themselves desperately crying out to God in extraordinarily difficult situations seems to me to be higher than it's ever been. I'm not making comment on big-picture things here; just a pastor noting the seeming uptick in crises in people's lives.

"…give me the discerning mind…" This thought, in the middle of this verse, is the one I want to reference a bit more, so we'll come back to it.

"…You promised…" A pretty common theme in Scripture: God has promised, in this case, a marvellous thing called a "discerning mind". Ponder that as you pray today…

Okay, to the "discerning mind". How timely is this; if there was ever a time that we need access to what God is thinking and doing, I would humbly suggest it's now! As I read that this morning, my mind immediately went to two other passages, both in the New Testament; 1 Corinthians 2:16 "Who can know the Lord's thoughts? Who knows enough to teach Him? But we understand these things, for we have the mind of Christ." And Romans 8:6 "So letting your sinful nature control your mind leads to death. But letting the Spirit control your mind leads to life and peace." There it is—one of the most beautiful realities of life as a believer; God promises to deeply partner with us in our minds, literally impacting the way we think! Let me express this as simply as I know how: the closer we walk with the Lord (getting "roots down" in Riverside language), the more deeply God influences, shapes and guides the way we think, resulting in more faith, more trust, more peace, more hope...

APPLICATION ▶ I think this is probably a "ponder" moment. No homework, no assignment...just ponder this magnificent concept...re-read the three scriptures we looked at today...

PRAYER

...and invite the Lord more deeply into the process.

"O Lord, listen to my cry; give me the discerning mind You have promised." So be it.

NINETY-ONE

WANDERING

SCRIPTURE ▶ Read Psalm 119:169-176.

OBSERVATION ▶ There are two tender little references in this last stanza that I'd like to ponder. Two actions that a good and kindly shepherd does as he cares for the sheep; two things that give us a beautiful insight into the heart of God; two things that might be missed in a quick read, but to those who have needed or experienced them, are precious and priceless!

Verse 173 says: "Give me a helping hand." Aren't you glad that our Shepherd is one who extends His hand when we ask? As I noted it's very simple, almost too simple. But what a powerful life truth is contained in that thought: when I need help and ask, He responds. Understanding this requires a couple of things; first, a childlikeness that steps into that thought simply, humbly and expectantly. Second, a growing and robust faith that recognizes that the help delivered is not necessarily instant, miraculous or profound—it is most often internal, quiet, and yet still deeply sustaining. It often takes a bit of time to adequately realize how significant His help has been.

The next little note is found in the very last verse of our journey through Psalm 119; verse 176. "I have wandered away like a lost sheep; come and find me." Who among us can't relate to that? Whether it was the "big wandering" in our lives before salvation, or the countless "little wanderings" of distractions, hurts and selfish missteps, the Good Shepherd has unfailingly

come after me to find me and tenderly bring me home. I'm
getting a little bit teary-eyed sitting here thinking about it…

***

APPLICATION   I'd suggest trying to remember instances in
your life when both or either of these actions of the Good
Shepherd have taken place. With thankfulness and humility, and
a growing sense of trust and affection for the Shepherd,
remember the truth of His loving actions toward you: the way
He cares by offering a helping hand, and the way He comes after
us when we wander away…

***

PRAYER

*Thank you, Lord, for the truth of Your Word. Thank you for
the faithful way that You have expressed your care and attention in
our lives. Help us to learn to quickly ask for help when we need it;
forgive us for the stubbornness we sometimes display. Thank you
that You always come after us when we wander away. More and
more, teach us to stay close… Amen. So be it.*

Blessings, dear friends…

NINETY-TWO

CHURCH

SCRIPTURE ▶   Read Psalm 122.

OBSERVATION ▶   "I was glad when they said to me, "Let us go to the house of the Lord." This well-known verse has been referenced many, many times in our collective experience through the years; either by a leader standing at the front of the church imploring a sleepy congregation to recognize the privilege of gathering together, or maybe as an individual trying to convince themselves to get out of a warm bed on a rainy Sunday morning and head out the door to church (just so you know, I, too, have actively participated in both of those scenarios!). Perhaps not seen in the reading of this passage is the context in which it was written. You'll notice that Psalms 120 through 134 all have the heading "A song for pilgrims ascending to Jerusalem". This group of psalms was therefore written by people who were heading to Jerusalem to worship and partner in a pilgrimage to the holy city. For some of them, it was a very rare journey, perhaps only once-in-a-lifetime; for it could be time-consuming, physically demanding and potentially very costly. Picture, if you will, a weary group of God-followers trudging through the largely barren countryside, inwardly wondering how much longer will this journey be? And then, rounding a corner,...Jerusalem appears! The beloved, beautiful, "house of the Lord"! After all of this time, after the rigorous demand of the pilgrimage, we finally made it! Can you imagine the growing excitement as they clamber up the final ascent to their destination? (Remember the heading: they are ascending to

Jerusalem.)

Their experience was probably not much like the modern church goer, who can basically attend church any time they want, oftentimes more of a matter of convenience than anything else. When they declared their gladness to go to the Temple, it was born out of a sense of deep sacrifice, weighty anticipation and intense longing. Again, sense the emotion contained in the next line (verse 2): "And now here we are, standing inside your gates, O Jerusalem", followed by a practical observation (verse 3) on the quality of the city's walls and construction (must have been composed by a carpenter or stone mason!).

All that to say: how are we doing at embracing the immense privilege we have to "go to the house of the Lord"? Has it become a chore? Does it lack a sense of anticipation and expectation? Have we perhaps neglected the beautiful purposes for which it was designed?

APPLICATION I can't answer those questions for you. I must answer them for myself on occasion, probably more frequently than you might imagine. Perhaps our application is as simple as this: re-read those first three verses, close your eyes, and imagine that incredible moment when the dream of worshipping in Jerusalem is realized...

PRAYER

...and pray something like this:

"Lord, thank you for the huge blessing of being able to go to your house. Help me to experience the miracle of the Church, your Body, to the fullest. Help me to prayerfully remember those who cannot go to your house, wherever they may be..." Amen.

Be blessed, dear friends...

NINETY-THREE

BUILDING OUR "HOUSE"

SCRIPTURE ▸ Read Psalm 127.

OBSERVATION ▸ I'm writing this a couple of days after the province I live in has experienced devastating flooding after a prolonged, intense, record-setting rainfall. We are all seeing images of severe property damage and the sorrow of people affected so greatly—it's truly a terrible thing to watch. Another thing that has happened as a result, and which is just coming into clearer focus, is the damage to the transportation infrastructure of the region; roadways, bridges, train tracks, drainage systems and the like. It will likely be quite a while until these things can be repaired and operational.

I write this as I read Psalm 127, especially verses 1&2. I can recall having heard these verses numerous times in the past, but they ring with certain poignancy today, as our province collectively ponders the fragility of the systems that we depend on so heavily. Few could have imagined the scope of ruin that was unleashed when the first raindrop of this storm fell to earth just a few days back. These verses are both illustration and a strong caution and this is so like our loving Father, a promise as well. The illustration comes in the form of a couple of pictures of residences, and the effort that goes into making them safe and livable. There's nothing inherently wrong with safety and livability—we all put some effort and expense into these things, and they bring us a degree of security. Next comes the caution; the risk of depending solely on human effort in any area of our lives. While it is prudent to take precautions and live and invest wisely, it can also become a trap; ultimately, a trap that will leave us exposed and lacking. "The work of the builders is wasted" and "guarding it with sentries will do no good" (v1) drive the point home. In a very material world, it is so easy to pursue human solutions and resources, at the expense of neglecting dependence on God, first and foremost. Finally, there is a promise found in verse 2, tacked on at the end of another caution: "It is useless for you to work so hard from early morning until late at night, anxiously working for food to eat; for God gives rest to His loved ones." (v2) What a comfort to us all; a comfort that is experienced by those who endeavour to trust God as life's highest priority. This is certainly not easy, and certainly not without missteps, but it is the great hope of God's beloved children; rest, provision and hope in the face of tremendous adversity and seeming despair all around.

APPLICATION ▶ Here's a thought: turn over to Matthew 7: 24-27 and have a read. Allow the Word to strengthen and encourage you as you continue to consider your heart's commitment to more deeply trust in God.

_____

_____

_____

_____

_____

_____

_____

PRAYER

I feel like our prayer should be twofold: first, for those around us who have suffered loss, that they would be comforted and provided for, and ultimately drawn to the Lord; and secondly, for the Lord's assistance in the building of our life's "house". We desperately need both.

_____

_____

_____

_____

_____

_____

_____

NINETY-FOUR
HEALTHY SPIRITUALITY

SCRIPTURE ▸   Read Psalm 131.

OBSERVATION ▸   I'm going to share something with you today that is very personal; something that gives you a glimpse into how I view and process what's going on in the world around us; something that could conceivably be misconstrued by some (I'm willing to take that risk), but also an action plan that I engage to keep myself focused and secure.

This psalm's author, David, was an extraordinary man. He was courageous (think Goliath), an outstanding leader (think leading armies and amassing a fortune in building materials for the Temple), supremely creative and artistic (think of the Psalms), and by all accounts, very intelligent. I add that last point because I think it's a necessary observation; he says something in verse 1 that could be misinterpreted as unintelligent at worst or juvenile at best. "I don't concern myself with matters too great" he writes, "or too awesome for me to grasp." He's writing there about a particular skill that I have found to be an immense help in my own spiritual journey—the ability to remain child-like in the face of extremely difficult circumstances. It's a mindset that Jesus Himself found quite appealing, even critically necessary in the lives and make-up of His followers. Remember His words in Matthew 18:3&4, in the midst of a discussion concerning 'greatness': "...unless you become like little children, you will never get into the Kingdom of Heaven."

King David had discovered that key to healthy spirituality. His life as a king was no doubt extremely complicated and demanding, and would have involved politics, conflict, finance and clashing cultures—weighty 'adult' matters, to be sure! And yet, in the face of the pressures and uncertainties kingship would bring, he had learned to set aside, even if fleetingly, its crushing demands and expectations. So, how did he do this? Verses 2 and 3 point the way: "Instead, I have calmed and quieted myself, like a weaned child who no longer cries for his mother's milk...", followed by the focal point of his efforts: "Put your hope in the Lord, now and always." The payoff was a childlikeness that can be disarming to some. I've heard the whispers before: "Why don't you care more? Why aren't you more concerned about what's going on around us?" Childlike rest is not about being ignorant or uninformed. It is rather an inner discipline that allows one to "calm and quiet" oneself, by focusing on the hope we find in the Lord. This is most usually experienced in the simple, disciplined acts of quiet moments with Jesus, time in the Word, worship and praise (Riversiders might remember the phrase "praise, not panic"...), spending time with other believers who are pursuing a similar sense. Nothing profound, nothing magical, nothing fancy or terribly impressive. Just the humble, trusting actions of a little child.

APPLICATION ▶ I think I kind of just shared a "to do" list of sorts. Check out the last paragraph again, take a deep breath, and set aside your concerns and focus your attention and affection on the Lord. Give it a bit of time and don't stop because you didn't sense or see an immediate change—keep at it!

PRAYER ▶

Lord, help me find that beautiful, healing, restful state of childlikeness. Draw my thoughts back to you when I find myself distracted or fearful. Teach me to know the joy and rest in the safety of your tender embrace. Amen.

Rest well, dear friends...

NINETY-FIVE

PRAISE THE LORD

SCRIPTURE Read Psalm 135.

OBSERVATION I was up early this morning. It was not a particularly special day. No big events, no pressing appointments, no real list of things to be accomplished. I didn't feel stressed out about anything, nor did I feel especially excited about any certain experience that lay before me. I had no discernible emotional position; not happy, not sad, not upset, not peaceful. Not sensing closeness to God, but not a distance either. It was a completely ordinary, unremarkable day. And then I opened my Bible to Psalm 135, and something struck me; something that literally changed the trajectory of my day. This psalm begins with a repeated call to praise (you'll note that the closing stanzas (verses 19-21) do the same). "Praise the Lord!" leapt off the page and accosted me and my thoughts.

And so I did. I sat in my leather recliner and began praising God. I took a few moments (that quickly grew into a few more moments!) and remembered the goodness and faithfulness of God. I started with myself and my own experiences and worked my way out, in an ever-expanding ripple of gratitude and remembrance. What quickly followed in the wake of that instruction to praise was this, and it happened quite unexpectedly, though quite forcefully: my inner man was lifted up. I could almost feel my chin rising, my sight and perspective being elevated. It happened with virtually no effort. It didn't feel forced or phony. It was a gift that naturally arrived, based on a response to a simple directive to praise the Lord. I noticed almost immediately a new sense of lightness, of optimism. Not because anything in my circumstances had noticeably changed—I had not left the house, not talked to anyone, not checked my emails, not watched the news…what had altered was in me, and it was producing something wonderful! What an amazing thing!

Some of you may be thinking "Well, that's pretty elementary, isn't it?", and I suppose you're right. Maybe an experienced believer like me should be practicing the discipline of praise every day, all day. Or perhaps the phrase "praise the Lord" has become so common, so trite, so over-used (if there is possibly such a thing!), so benign, that I've lost a sense of its truth and power… Nevertheless, I was deeply affected by taking some time to praise the Lord. It was liberating, encouraging and strengthening, and it all took place in a few minutes, in my favourite chair, in the dark of the morning, with no one in sight.

_____

_____

_____

_____

_____

_____

_____

APPLICATION If you need a little assist to begin your own personal 'praise therapy', read through the verses in between the opening and closing admonitions in the passage. The psalmist does an excellent job of describing the awesomeness of God, both past and present; recalling His goodness (v3), His greatness (v5), His purposefulness (v6&7), His power (v8-10), His generosity (v12), and His compassion (v14).

PRAYER

Praise the Lord! Blessings, dear friends...

NINETY-SIX

HIS FAITHFUL LOVE

SCRIPTURE ▶ Read Psalm 136.

OBSERVATION ▶ Here's a tough one: quickly read Psalm 136 and then immediately state the main theme!

In the entire Bible, I don't think that there's another passage that is so utterly repetitive, so committed to a single theme: "His faithful love endures forever." Twenty-six verses; twenty-six mentions. Do you suppose that God is trying to tell us something?

A couple of thoughts about the statement "His faithful love endures forever". His love is faithful. It will never run out, never leave, never waver, never forget. What a comfort that is! No matter what situation we find ourselves in, His love remains faithful. This theme is consistent throughout the Word (have a quick review of 1 Corinthians 13 to further clarify the beauty and power of His faithful love), and has most certainly been spoken by countless people, many in unbelievably dire life circumstances, across the broad expanse of human history. It has held the people of God steady when empires have collapsed, wars have raged, tragedy has struck, and natural disasters have ravaged the earth. His faithful love… Other systems, internal and external, will fail, such as governments, education, science, medicine and technology—they can only deliver finite results. Relationships will sometimes break, death will interrupt the happiest of families, and organizations will disappoint; human nature has a way of guaranteeing that. Only God can make that claim: My faithful love will endure forever!

And then there's the 'forever' part: our eternity! That's no small consideration! While it remains difficult, maybe impossible, to imagine an eternal existence after death, this declaration from God doesn't blink in its certainty: there is a never-ending love embrace that God promises to His beloved children. I don't think the point here is to attempt to describe heaven; for me, the attempts to do so are more of a distraction than any real practical help, as wonderful as they may be. God seems content to use a minimalist approach: it's all about love, and all about forever—'nuff said.

APPLICATION May you, too, experience the quiet inner comfort that comes from the unfailing love of your Heavenly Father, no matter what you're going through right now. Most assuredly, that can be your experience today—the faithful love of God supporting and encouraging you on your journey. Slow things down for a moment or two and contemplate the enormity of that statement: His faithful love endures forever! Pick a couple of the verses that stand out to you from Psalm 136 and let them settle over you.

If you have never made a personal expression of receiving God's faithful love for you (for that is how you can actually experience the life-changing reality of His love), you can do that very simply in this moment…something like this:

_____

_____

_____

_____

_____

_____

_____

PRAYER

> *God, I want to know your faithful, never-ending love in my life. I accept your gift of love, shown in the person of your Son, Jesus. Wash away my mistakes, take away my aloneness, heal my pain, and fill me with your love forever. Amen. "His faithful love endures forever."*
>
> *Bless you, dear friends…*

_____

_____

_____

_____

_____

_____

NINETY-SEVEN

RICH FOOD

SCRIPTURE Read Psalm 138.

OBSERVATION I write this in the first week of December, as Advent and Christmas come ever more into view. While my opening thought about this psalm is not particularly 'spiritual', it may be useful in helping us to partake richly and fully in it. Here goes…

In my life's experience, the Christmas season often has expressions of food and eating, sometimes excessively so! My favourite has always been the smorgasbord; approaching the food table, empty plate in hand, then progressively loading up with favourites (and knowing the inner satisfaction of rejecting the less appetizing dishes); gazing and grazing over the selections before you and personalizing your own meal from the bounty spread before you. It's that part of the smorgasbord that I want to reflect on, in light of Psalm 138. As I read this passage, I had that familiar sensation: so many good things presented before me that I hardly know where to start! (I know this may have been a bit of a stretch, but I'm determined to make it work!) Here's a sampling of the rich and hearty meal that is presented (each of which is worth a second helping…sorry, I couldn't resist…)

- ◆ v1: the 'meal' begins with praise and thankfulness. This is always a great start to prayer and friendship with God.
- ◆ v2: a tremendous insight that produces encouragement and faith. "…your promises are backed by all the honour of your

name." Recall a promise that God has given you and speak
verse 2 to yourself and your situation!

- ◆ v3: an insight into the processes of prayer, of the interaction
  between God and His children. We pray; He answers, He
  encourages us, He strengthens us…
- ◆ v5: a reminder about proper focus: directed to God and His
  glory, not to me and my difficulties.
- ◆ v6: a teaching reminder about pride and humility, that we
  regularly need; it keeps us safe, and properly aligned with
  our Father.
- ◆ v7: a promise to put into practice—thanks, Lord!
- ◆ v8: a lifetime observation, both a promise and a Word-inspired
  hope, a powerful faith-builder: "The Lord will work out His
  plans for my life—for your faithful love endures forever."

No matter where you are, what you're going through, or
what your challenges are—the Lord is committed to fulfilling
His plans for you! Now, that is worth a second helping, for sure!

APPLICATION ▶   I hope my somewhat corny illustration was
of some help to you. My suggestion, in keeping with today's
'smorgasbord' theme, is to head back to the buffet and read

through the passage again, slowly and thoughtfully. Let the Lord direct you to what selections you need most.

PRAYER

Lord, thanks for the richness of your Word. Thank you for your many, many promises. Teach me to slow down and trust; to remember well your faithfulness throughout my life. To find my hope and strength in You...amen.

Bless you, dear friends...

NINETY-EIGHT

INTIMACY WITH GOD

SCRIPTURE ▶   Read Psalm 139.

OBSERVATION ▶   Have you ever seen a movie, read a book, or gone to an event that was so brilliant, so exquisite, and so breathtaking, that words failed you as you tried to describe it to someone afterwards? I have that same sense of wonderful helplessness as I ponder Psalm 139! In fact, I can even recall throughout my life, moments when someone has simply used the words "Psalm 139" as a catch-all descriptor of the goodness and majesty of God—usually with a little shrug of the shoulders, a slight tilt of the head, and a smile. I think what strikes me, and shapes my outlook most, is the intimacy with which God knows His children.

The first six verses could be read as a "first thing in the morning" devotional, literally every day of our lives, and its reminder would never get old! There is not a moment of my existence, not a movement, not a thought, not a simple action, not a tear, not a single situation that is not tenderly watched by our Heavenly Father. Matthew 10:29-31 comes to mind from my childhood: "...not a single sparrow can fall to the ground without your Father knowing it. And the very hairs on your head are numbered. So don't be afraid; you are more valuable to God than a whole flock of sparrows." What a comfort, what a tender reminder; and so very necessary in our human journey, when so often we can feel abandoned or alone. Praise God for His "hand of blessing on my head." (v5) Verse six captures the overwhelming wonder of God's loving attention perfectly: "Such knowledge is too wonderful for me, too great for me to understand!" In other words, words fail me!

The verses that follow echo the sentiments of God's infinite and intimate kindness and care in our lives.

- (v7): "I can never get away from your presence." What hope that inspires, for ourselves and for those we know who have wandered away from the Lord!
- (v8-12) The majestic poetic imagery of "riding the wings of the morning" and asking "the darkness to hide me" to describe God's relentless pursuit of His beloved children.
- (v13-18) Intimacy articulated.
- (v19-22) He even understands my anger, frustration, and disappointment.
- (v23-24) A closing word for life today: "Search me, O God, and know my heart; test me and know my anxious thoughts." He is acutely aware of my fears and my anxieties, and dedicates Himself to leading me safely home...

APPLICATION How about this for a challenge: for the next seven days, read Psalm 139: 1-6, first thing in the morning, and last thing before bedtime. I'll commit to do the same; together, let's see how we'll be impacted by the power and truth of the Word.

_____

_____

_____

_____

_____

_____

_____

_____

PRAYER

Speak out verses 23 and 24; let those words form your prayer. Bless you, dear friends...

_____

_____

_____

_____

_____

_____

_____

NINETY-NINE
WORSHIPPING WELL

SCRIPTURE ▶ Read Psalm 145.

OBSERVATION ▶ At the risk of sounding old and outdated, I'd like to share a thought about worship from the church experience of my spiritually formative years. Upon reading Psalm 145, I was reminded of how much the songs we sang in worship way back then came directly from the Word. It seems to me that perhaps there was a deeper commitment to utilize the Bible itself as a guide to worship, as opposed to something to be only studied and read; the emphasis tended to be less on personal experience and the feelings that might accompany that, and more on simply declaring the truth of scripture, using musical worship as the vehicle. I can even remember times when the rhythm and meter of the words didn't quite align with the melody, but it didn't seem to matter that much!

That's the sense I had today as I read Psalm 145: it was like an unbroken expression of praise, and every line or stanza seemed like it should be sung or shouted in praise, which I suspect is a reflection of David the musician and psalmist. Here's a couple of 'for examples':

(Note the use of the mouth and voice in the act of worship, and the communal nature of worship.)

- ◆ vs 4: "Let each generation tell its children of your mighty acts…"

- ◆ vs 6: "Your awe-inspiring deeds will be on every tongue; I will proclaim your greatness."
- ◆ vs 7: "Everyone will share the story of your wonderful goodness; they will sing with joy about your righteousness."
- ◆ vs 10,11: "…and your faithful followers will praise you. They will speak of the glory of your kingdom; they will give examples of your power."

And so on, and so on…

APPLICATION I'm certainly not here to advocate the dismantling of modern worship in favour of a return to something from the past. Many have been the times where the current corporate expression of worship has brought health, wholeness and healing to my life. I guess my points are simple enough, and really just circle back to the personal responsibility and privilege that every believer is entrusted with in regards to the 'heart' condition of our worship lives. First, don't be timid in utilizing your Bible in praise and worship of the Lord. This might appear mostly in your own quiet devotional times, but certainly could be applied to moments in which you are singing a song and scripture underlines truth in that song—be watching for it! It is, after all, straight from the Source! Second, don't forget to worship in community. There is something undeniably powerful and transformative about worshipping together. In other words, go to church! As an exercise today, read through this Psalm and feel the songs of praise and adoration rise up in you!

PRAYER

Lord, help me in my desire to more deeply and more fully worship you. Help me to get my eyes off myself and my circumstances, and to focus on You. Compose in me a new song of worship!

ONE HUNDRED

COMPETING VOICES

SCRIPTURE Read Psalm 146 &147.

OBSERVATION One of the most challenging things we've all encountered in the past couple of years is the many, many loud voices competing for people's attention, each seemingly convinced that they alone have a corner on the truth. In all honesty, it's been hard sometimes to know who to listen to, and who to steer clear of.

Nestled among the faith-building statements found in these two Psalms are a couple of really helpful, steadying observations about the humanness (read: unreliability) of many of the voices around us that clamour for an audience, and through those simple observations, a way to clarify the choices and priorities to be embraced in pursuit of a faith-based life. Each chapter contains one helpful caution:

- Psalm 146:3 says: "Don't put your confidence in powerful people; there is no help for you there."
- Psalm 147:10 phrases it this way: "He (God) takes no pleasure in the strength of a horse or in human might." In other words, the problem is not so much in listening well, taking advice, making decisions, and responding to outside voices with prayerful and reasonable rationality. To do less would be foolish—after all, we know that God largely places governments and authorities in our lives to benefit us. The problem comes more with prioritizing those voices, and this is really a personal determination

of where our ultimate allegiances lie. To what degree do human wisdom, human resources and human provision take precedence in my life? Have they become the unquestioned source of my life existence? Do they ever crowd out truth, faith and love? Do they ever pressure me to compromise my commitments to the Lord? That's really the essence of faith in God: a deep inner sense that, at the end of the day, my choices have been made; I believe in God as my source, my provider, my hope. It is His voice that I long for and depend on, above all others, even though popular opinion might say otherwise.

_____

_____

_____

_____

_____

_____

_____

_____

_____

_____

APPLICATION Now, admittedly, this can be a little tricky; after all, these types of commitments are not generally made in a one-time surge of emotion at the end of a church service. These things are proven over the course of time; much time to be exact, with plenty of room for wavering, faltering and weakness of faith. So, where to start? You could start by slowly reading these two Psalms again and noting the times that God's faithfulness and trustworthiness are mentioned—that act alone will build your faith, and by extension, your commitment level to Him. Remember, this will take time, but the long-term, repetitive, faithful investment of these "heart" principles will predictably bear the beautiful fruit of increased trust and desirable fruit. And that, my friends, is ultimately what Christian living looks like.

PRAYER

Lord, we really need your assistance here. There are so many voices competing for our attention, and ultimately, our allegiance. Help me to hear You well; help me to grow in faith and trust. Grant me the desire to know You, to experience You, to hear You, to obey You. Amen; So be it.

Bless you, dear friends...

ONE HUNDRED & ONE
PRAISE-WORTHY!

SCRIPTURE Read Psalm 148.

OBSERVATION What's the difference between 'praise' and 'worship'? The two words are liberally used throughout the Bible, and would still be recognizable to most in the Church today. The term 'worship' has probably become more closely associated with the musical expression that we would experience on a Sunday morning, though segments of that could be reasonably described as 'praise'. I could at this point simply go to a dictionary and pass that information along. Or, I could look into one of numerous excellent books on the subject (Jack Hayford's "Glory on Your House", being a personal favourite); instead, after reading through Psalm 148, I will give you some of my thoughts and observations gleaned through the years.

As is recorded in this Psalm (11 times) I will focus mostly on praise, with a few worship-related tidbits thrown in. First off, I don't believe the point is to belabour the distinctions, as much as it is to practice the concept, the over-arching principle being that we are encouraged to emulate the entirety of creation by engaging in the exaltation of God. Certainly, both 'praise' and 'worship' fall under that umbrella. For me, the simplest distinction is probably that I see 'praise' as more of an action, while 'worship' speaks of an attitude. The style, exuberance, posture, or expression (outward or inward) are really not terribly important discussion points for me, though I admit I still have much to learn here. One of my biggest challenges has been the tendency I have to judge people's sincerity via the expressiveness of their praise and worship (this is not always helped by pastoring a Spirit-filled church). This is not a new problem, as the stories of Hannah and Eli (1Samuel) and also the immediate aftermath of outpouring of the Holy Spirit (Acts 2) remind us; deeply reverential travail in the Spirit (worship?) in the case of Hannah, and exuberant declaration (praise?) in the experience of the followers of Jesus upon receiving the infilling of the Holy Spirit. Both of which were initially attributed to the effects of too much alcohol!

So, where do we go from here? Psalm 148 lists a string of "created things" (v5) that are encouraged to praise their Creator, which they evidently and naturally do. Toward the end of the chapter, the admonition to praise changes from 'things' and begins to encourage 'people' (v 11&12) to follow suit; this is where it gets personal and practical for us, because it now becomes an act of the will, which is where we have decisions to make regarding our engagement.

APPLICATION▶   Really the point of composing (another!) devotional book comes down to a moment such as this. Especially for someone like me, who is designed and assigned to 'pastor' people, in other words, to move them from one place to another, presumably in the pursuit of knowing God more deeply. Strategic opportunities to apply scripture in order to facilitate growth, intimacy and experiential understanding are everything! I believe our inner beings would be strengthened today by a re-read of Psalm 148, maybe with pencil and paper at the ready, in order to list the things about the Lord that make Him praise-worthy. (I've been working on my list as I wrote this; much of my praise has been focused on His faithful guidance and provision.) So, I suppose whether you define the active relationship you experience with the Lord as expressing itself through 'praise' or through 'worship', I think the application is, like Nike advised us: "Just do it".

PRAYER

Let my prayer take the form of praise today—so much is actually asked and answered when we do!

"Kings of the earth and all people, rulers and judges of the earth, young men and young women, old men and children. Let them all praise the name of the Lord." (148:11-13)

*If you are looking to begin your journey
with Jesus, we would recommend starting with
something like this:*

*"Jesus, I invite you into my heart.
Please forgive my sins, and make yourself at home.*

*I believe that You are God's Son;
I believe that you died on the cross to forgive the
sins of the world (including mine) and
that you rose from the dead.*

Teach me how to live with you living in my heart.

Thank you that you'll never leave me alone."

If you prayed that prayer to invite Jesus into
your heart, or would simply like to connect
with someone at Riverside Community
Church, please visit the church's website
at *rside.ca.*

Riverside Community Church is located in
Port Coquitlam, B.C. Canada, and is part of
the Foursquare Gospel Church of Canada.

Manufactured by Amazon.ca
Bolton, ON

40493108R00152